THE KIDS' HOW TO DO (ALMOST) Everything GUIDE

Edited by Murray Suid
Illustrated by Philip Chalk

This book is for
Ronald and Kirsten

Publisher: Roberta Suid
Designer: Susan Pinkerton
Copy Editor: Carol Whiteley
Production: Scott McMorrow
Cover: Philip Chalk

Philip Chalk drawn by Philip Chalk

Other Monday Morning publications by the editor include:
How to Be an Inventor, *How to Be President of the U.S.A.*,
Storybooks Teach Writing, and *Ten-Minute Grammar Grabbers*

Online address: MMBooks@aol.com
Web address: www.mondaymorningbooks.com

For a complete catalog, write to the address above.

Jonathan Vos Post's "How to Talk to an Extraterrestrial" (pages 174 and 175) is adapted from his "Me Human, You Alien: How to Talk to an Extraterrestrial," published in *Making Contact: a Serious Handbook for Locating and Communicating with Extraterrestrials*, edited by Bill Fawcett (William Morrow, 1997).

ISBN 1-57612-046-5
Printed in the United States of America
9 8 7 6 5 4 3 2 1

CONTENTS

INTRODUCTION

No matter how smart we are, we can always get smarter. One way this can happen is by learning surprising facts. For example, did you know that mice and giraffes have the same number of neck bones? That's a fact, and now it's in your brain. A second way to get smarter is by developing skills, such as making a telescope or drawing funny cartoon characters.

Although both ways of becoming smarter are important and work together, *The Kids' How to Do (Almost) Everything Guide* focuses on skill building. Here, you'll learn everything from how to act in movies to how to avoid shark attacks.

TAKE IT FROM EXPERTS

A good way to master any skill is to study with an expert. If you want to invent things, get advice from a successful inventor. If you want to play music, find a musician. If you want to build a boat, look for a boat builder. Experts understand skills from the inside out.

This book is written *entirely* by experts, such as Alison Fujino, who wrote the lesson on boomerangs. She hasn't just read about boomerangs: she is a boomerang champion! Likewise, James Morrow, who will teach you how to write fiction, spends hours a day turning out prize-winning stories.

Other experts contributing to this book include:
- a doctor
- a puppeteer
- a prize-winning sand sculptor
- an adventurer who walked to the South Pole
- a travel photographer
- a soccer coach
- a roller coaster critic
- an actress who does voices for animated movies
- a children's book author
- a sportswriter
- a Mongolian camel rider

TODAY...

Many of the lessons can be used immediately:

• If you want to publish on the Web, follow the steps outlined by Web master Elnora Chambers.

• If something is broken around your house, read engineer Scott McMorrow's tips about fixing things.

• If you're planning a trip and can't fit everything into your suitcase, you'll find answers from world-traveler Betty Winsett.

• If you're scheduled to give a speech but tremble with stage fright, worry no more. Study the proven fear-fighting strategies shared by Wanda Lincoln, who has given lectures throughout the world.

...AND TOMORROW

This book also describes activities that require time to learn. For example, chess master Peter Kurzdorfer tells how to sharpen your chess skills. But to get really good, you must practice. This is also true for becoming a clown, doing stand-up comedy, riding a horse, speaking a new language, and solving math problems. Luckily, practice can be fascinating and fun.

WEB-EXTENDED

This book is Web-Extended™, which means that it's interactive. Using an online computer (your own or perhaps one in a library or school), connect to the Internet, go to www.mondaymorningbooks.com, and click the Web-Extended icon. This will take you to an area where you can ask us questions, discover how the book was put together, find additional materials, share your ideas with other readers, and tell us other skills you'd like to learn.

We hope you have a good time trying the lessons and getting smarter every day.

Murray Suid
Palo Alto, California
Msuid@aol.com

PART 1

THE ARTS

HOW TO Be a Movie Actor
—by Ned Vaughn

Being a movie actor is exciting! You get to travel to exotic locations and work with creative people. On the other hand, the business can be very tough. When you start out, you'll try for many parts, but usually not be chosen. Early in my career, I got one job for every thirty auditions. Now the odds are about one in ten. Auditioning is still a struggle, but when I see myself in a movie, it's worth it. If you're interested in shooting for the stars, just follow your dreams . . . and the tips below.

DIRECTIONS

1. Go on stage. When I was eight, I tried out for a part in a local production of *Oliver!* I got a small role, and I discovered I loved acting. This led to taking parts in many plays during my school years.

2. Take acting classes. I learned a lot about acting on my own by watching movies and by paying attention to people, including myself. But I became a serious actor after taking an acting course in college. Later I moved to New York and studied acting full time. I began to master a variety of technical skills. For example, one of my classes was called "Fencing for Actors."

3. Develop non-acting skills. Scripts often call for actors with special talents, such as martial arts, skiing, sailing, diving, or surfing. Sometimes, landing a role requires that you take intensive training, for example, learning to ride a horse to play a cowboy. But it can be a big plus if you can juggle, scuba dive, or whatever.

continued ...

4. Work on accents. I'm from the South and can speak with a southern accent. But learning other accents increases my odds for getting parts.

5. Prepare a "package." This consists of a head shot done as an 8 x 10 inch photograph (20 cm x 25 cm) with a résumé attached to the back. The résumé lists the acting jobs you've had. You might also include a short video of your work.

6. Get an agent. A talent agent finds roles that match your talents, and helps you get interviewed or "tested." Without an agent, getting work is much harder. Agents are listed in the phone book and in industry reference books. You may need to visit many agents before one accepts you. The agent receives ten percent of your pay.

7. Prepare for an audition. You'll get a script a day or two ahead of time. Read the entire script. This will help you understand your part. Rehearse your scenes by having someone read the lines of other characters in the scenes. If you have time, memorizing your lines can be very helpful.

8. Don't expect quick success. Acting is a competitive business. Some successful actors tried for years before getting their first job.

9. Help your fellow actors. When you get a movie job, you'll probably rehearse a scene several times with the other actors. During the rehearsal, you may get an idea for action that could be done by a fellow actor. If the actor seems open, share your thought.

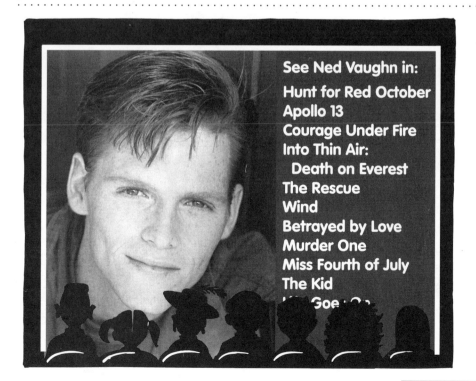

See Ned Vaughn in:

Hunt for Red October
Apollo 13
Courage Under Fire
Into Thin Air:
 Death on Everest
The Rescue
Wind
Betrayed by Love
Murder One
Miss Fourth of July
The Kid

Ned Vaughn has appeared in many films, and also spent a year on the TV series *China Beach*.

HOW TO Make Your Puppet Come Alive

—by John W. Higgins

Puppets are wonderful, magical creatures that love to play with us. But they need us to help them come alive. I've been playing and working for many years with my puppet friend Obieyoyo. Here's what I've learned that can help you bring your puppet friends to life.

DIRECTIONS

1. Find a puppet. Store-bought puppets are fine, or you can make puppets from a paper bag or a sock. For the bag and the sock, you'll need to color or paste on eyes and a nose.

2. Get to know the puppet by looking at it eye-to-eye. Is it a girl? A boy? A troll? A monster? Can you imagine what it's thinking right now? Is the puppet mean? Friendly? Happy?

3. Notice how the puppet makes you feel. Does its face make you want to laugh? Sing? Shout? Whisper? Good—you're getting an idea of what the puppet's personality is like.

4. Create a voice for the puppet. Open the puppet's mouth while you speak for it. What is the voice like? Low? High? Squeaky? You're on your way to having your puppet come alive.

5. Now try out all kinds of different voices and characters for your puppet. Be creative and go wild! Soon you'll discover just how your new puppet pal talks, thinks, feels—just like when you first meet a real-live, human friend.

continued ...

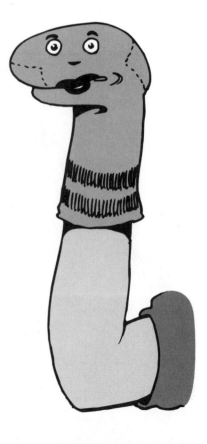

6. If you have two or more puppets, experiment with all of them. You'll soon see that each is very different from the others. After you play with puppets for a while, you'll find that you won't need to think about how they talk, or what they're going to say next. They'll start talking for themselves—with your help, of course.

7. If your puppets want to perform on a stage, you can make one for them. Try putting a broomstick across the backs of two chairs, with the chair backs facing each other. Then put a towel or sheet over the broomstick. Or turn a big cardboard box upside down with a hole cut out for the stage. Even easier, just go hide behind the couch and let the puppet play on top of the back. Ask your puppet friend where he or she or it likes to play.

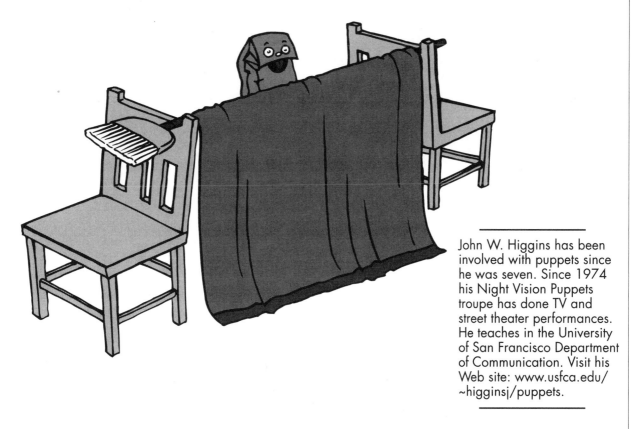

John W. Higgins has been involved with puppets since he was seven. Since 1974 his Night Vision Puppets troupe has done TV and street theater performances. He teaches in the University of San Francisco Department of Communication. Visit his Web site: www.usfca.edu/ ~higginsj/puppets.

HOW TO Be a CLOWN
—by Marc P. Summers

clown (*pronounced klown*) *1. a comic entertainer, especially in pantomime or circus, usually with traditional costume and make-up. 2. a silly, foolish, or playful person. 3. a jester, joker, funny man or woman.*

The above definition teaches us that a clown should entertain, be humorous, and portray joy and happiness. To do so, a clown must look like fun.

A professional clown will take up to 45 minutes to put on make-up before a show. In addition to face painting, this time is used for trying on different expressions: smiling, looking surprised, sad, happy, and so on until the performer feels the character he or she is going to play.

I love it when friends see me as a clown and ask, "Is that really you?" This means that I have disguised myself so well that even friends have trouble recognizing me. If you'd like to have the same experience, let's see what we can do with your face and your whole self.

DIRECTIONS

1. Get to know your face. Stand before a mirror and draw your face. Or, if you find it easier, trace a photograph. Now look in the mirror and watch what happens when you smile, raise your eyebrows, and so on. You'll notice that your face moves in different ways. Next, with colored pens draw clown features on the top of your original drawing. Be creative. If you have a small mouth, you can make it larger with an outline. You can highlight eyes and completely transform your face.

continued ...

2. Paint your real face. Using the picture you drew as a model, apply face paints to your real face. While in front of the mirror, try on various expressions to see how your "design face" moves.

3. Dress up. Now you need to find some suitable clothing. Most clowns wear oversized clothing. Try to find some old baggy trousers (pants) that aren't needed anymore, and then look for scraps of colored material. Perhaps with some help from someone who's good at tailoring, cut the material into squares and sew them onto the trousers. Do the same with a baggy shirt. Presto, you now have a clown face and a simple clown costume.

4. Prepare a few clowning tricks. When I do a show, I start off wearing nothing on my feet. After introducing myself, I ask my audience whether they notice what item of clothing I have forgotten. After a while of looking up and down, the whole audience starts shouting, "Shoes!" I then say, "Silly me" and go into my large suitcase and get out two beach spades (shovels), and slip my feet through the handles. It doesn't take long for the audience to shout, "They're not shoes." Again, I go into my case to find my size 17 clown shoes. I put them on my hands and say, "OK, let's start the show." Eventually I end up with both shoes on one foot, and then both shoes on the correct feet but tied together, and fall all over the stage.

This example shows that you can use simple everyday actions to make people laugh. Try to think of something that you do regularly that you could use in your clown act. For example, if you walk your dog daily, how about a skit in which you walk an imaginary dog? Other possible clowning actions include cleaning your teeth, making your bed, washing dishes, or playing a sport.

Marc P. Summers, alias Pancake the Clown, is the only clown in England to have a Diploma of Clownology from the United States of America. He studied at the Texas Clown School in Houston. He clowns at birthday parties, and other celebrations.

HOW TO Create  Picture Books

—by Leslie Tryon

My passion is storytelling with pictures. Although every picture book that I create is different, I always follow the same steps. Other authors may do the job differently. But this is my way, and perhaps it will help you tell and draw your stories.

DIRECTIONS

1. Get an idea. You can forget all the rest if you don't have a good idea. My ideas usually come from life—from the things I see and do. For example, because I have spent so much time on stage as a dancer and as a performer, it's not surprising that I would write *Albert's Play*.

2. Draft the story. Although I'm an illustrator, for me the story is the book's foundation. The story must be able to stand on its own. Good pictures cannot save weak words. Usually, I will rewrite many times before I'm satisfied with the manuscript.

3. Make a storyboard. After I have written the story, I draw a storyboard. This consists of tiny pictures called "thumbnails" that give a sense of what readers will see on each page of the book. I redo the storyboard many times to get it right. My goal is to see if the story works overall.

4. Share the story. At this point, I'm still shaping the book, so I don't want detailed feedback. But it's helpful to find out if someone else likes the idea. I always show my work to my editor at the company that publishes my books. But I also ask friends for their reactions.

continued ...

5. Draw each illustration full size. I have a visual memory, plus a strong imagination. Still, I often draw from real life. Several of my characters are based on pets in my neighborhood. I use photos for reference but never draw directly from them.

6. Build a model if needed. To draw a complex object from several perspectives, I'll first build a three-dimensional model.

7. Combine the drawings and words in a preliminary book, known as a "dummy." I'll share this with my editor and with a few friends who may point out parts that need improving.

8. Create final art. I trace a clean pencil sketch from each preliminary drawing. The sketch goes onto paper that's specially made for ink, watercolors, and other media. I may spend six months completing a few dozen pages.

9. Add the type. The final look of the page depends a lot on the typeface you use and how you place it. In professional publishing, this work is done by a specialist called a book designer. But anyone with access to a computer and a publishing program can experiment with typography.

10. Design the cover. The cover is a key part of a book because it invites readers inside. Sometimes my editor and I go through many ideas before we get a cover that we both like. It even happens that we'll change the title of the book at the last minute.

11. Make copies and bind the pages. For a professional picture book, this can take three months. But at a copy shop, you can make copies of a handmade book in only minutes.

Leslie Tryon has written and illustrated many children's books, including *Albert's Alphabet*, *Albert's Christmas*, and *Albert's Ballgame*.

HOW TO Draw Animal CARTOONS
—by Mike Artell

Cartooning is fun even if you're not a great artist. You can use cartoons to illustrate stories, books, posters, flyers, greeting cards, invitations, and whatever needs an eye-catching visual. Here are some ideas for creating cartoon animals.

DIRECTIONS

1. Decide what kind of animal you want to draw.
Do you want to draw something big and heavy like an elephant? Or would you rather draw something little and cute like a mouse or a bug? It's up to you!

2. Do research.
Try to observe the animal you want to draw. Birds, bugs, dogs, and cats are almost everywhere. Animals like elephants can be found in zoos or on television nature shows.
- Watch how the animal stands and how it moves.
- Watch how it eats.
- Look at it from several different points of view.
- Read books about the animal you want to draw.

Learn something about the animal. Later, this will help you to exaggerate its features and give it some personality.

3. Make a rough sketch of your animal.
This is to help you get more familiar with it. The trick is to make quick drawings of the animal without trying to make your drawings perfect. Sometimes it's hard to make yourself draw quickly because you want to draw the animal the "right" way. Instead, just draw the basic animal shape and add a few details. Stay loose. Remember, this is only a sketch.

continued ...

4. Make new sketches that exaggerate a part of your animal. If the creature has a big beak, give it a BIG, BIG beak. If it has many legs, give it LOTS AND LOTS of legs. If it has small eyes, give it tiny eyes. This is the point where your sketch becomes a cartoon. Keep in mind that you're creating "fun art," not "fine art," so relax.

5. Give the cartoon animal personality. One way to do this is to have it do "people" activities. For example:

• A beaver's flat tail resembles a tennis racket. So draw a beaver playing tennis with its tail.

• A giraffe's long neck lets it eat leaves off tall trees. That neck would also come in handy if the giraffe wanted to slam dunk a basketball. It could take the ball in its mouth and WHAM! Two points!

6. List your animal's characteristics to help you think up funny situations. The settings and problems you give your animal will be as important as how funny you make it look. Think about situations before you draw your final cartoon.

7. Draw your final cartoon based on your sketches. Remember that a cartoon should amuse the reader. You're not trying to draw pictures that look like photographs. A great cartoon relies on everything working together: the drawing, the situation, and your sense of humor.

As you can see, it's just as important to THINK funny as it is to DRAW funny. If you experiment with different situations, exaggerate the characteristics of your animals, and add your own unique sense of humor, you're sure to create great animal cartoons.

Mike Artell is an award-winning children's book author and illustrator. His books include *Legs, Starry Skies,* and *Writing Start-ups.* Each year, Mike visits many schools to lead drawing and writing workshops. His e-mail address is: MikeArtell@aol.com.

HOW TO Make ORIGAMI
—by Nick Robinson

To make best use of this guide, find yourself a simple origami book and some paper, then read on!

DIRECTIONS

1. When to fold. Choose a suitable time and place to fold. Peace and quiet help; it's very difficult to make perfect origami with distractions all around you. Music helps some people concentrate. With more difficult designs, you may need several sessions to complete a fold. In any case, if you start to feel tense or annoyed, it's best to take a break. A good night's rest will often work wonders.

2. Where to fold. Origami masters fold in the air, so they can feel both sides of the paper at once. This is fun to watch but will cause problems for the beginner, since neat creases are harder to make. It's best to start by using a table to fold on. Having the diagrams and paper in front of you encourages you to take your time between folds to study the next instruction.

3. Fold to an edge. It's much easier to fold to an edge of the paper than to a crease, which can sometimes be hard to see. A paper edge allows you to line things up accurately. If a fold is easier made by turning the paper around or upside down, then do it! Turn the paper back afterwards so that it matches the next diagram. Check a few steps ahead of yourself to see what you're aiming for. That way, even if you are not sure, you may be able to complete the step and then work out how you did it!

continued …

Make an origami bookmark!

1.

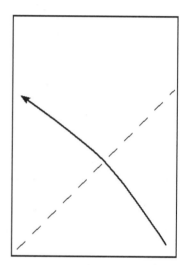

2.

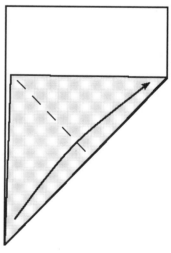

4. Line up before creasing. Before making firm creases, make sure that the paper is lined up exactly where it should be; badly positioned creases can be adjusted, but will make the folding far more difficult and spoil the clean lines of the final result. A small mistake made at the beginning will also seem bigger at the end. Be especially careful with corners; they often end up as "points" such as feet, beaks, or tails. Careless folding may lead to a bird with no beak!

5. Work at it. As with most hobbies, some people will find origami easier than others. If you find it hard, slow down a bit and choose simple designs to start with—practice makes perfect! Your first attempts at origami may look a bit untidy. The next time it will be easier and you'll do a neater job. Sometimes you'll make a dozen figures before one really looks good. With really difficult designs, you may get so far, then have to give up. Try again the next day; you'll get there eventually. If you fold with friends, you can help each other through the difficult stages, as well as share new designs!

6. If at first you don't succeed.... Origami is usually a peaceful, relaxing pursuit, but sometimes the paper can appear so unhelpful you feel like throwing it in the nearest bin. This is quite normal, so don't be put off! The paper will do as it's told, but you have to ask politely! In many cases your problem will be either poor creasing or misunderstanding the instructions. The key is to take your time. Try not to force the paper into position (unless the instructions tell you too!), but try to fold it gently, creasing only when you are certain.

Above all, enjoy your origami!

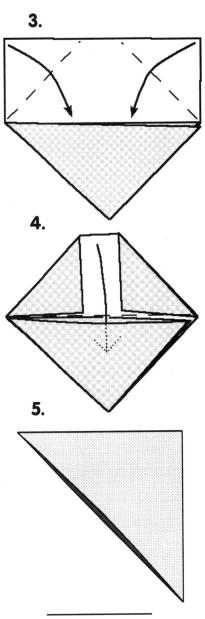

Nick Robinson is an English musician and lecturer in Information Technology. He has folded all manner of things since discovering origami in 1982. He has written a book on paper airplanes. He can be reached via his Web site: http://www.rpmrecords.co.uk/bos/.

HOW TO Publish on the WEB
—by Elnora Chambers

When you see all the cool stuff that's available on the Internet, you might think making Web pages is impossibly difficult. It isn't. If you are patient and can type accurately, you can share your ideas with people around the world.

Web publishing involves adding HTML "tags" to your text. HTML stands for Hypertext Mark-up Language. These tags tell computers how to display the words when a person views the pages on the Internet. You can buy software that automatically adds HTML tags. But by learning to add the tags yourself, you'll have a better understanding of how Web pages work.

And what about pictures? The final page of this lesson tells how to add them to your Web page.

DIRECTIONS

1. Open a new document with your text editor. Do not use a word processing program.

2. Type the text you want on your Web page. Don't worry about font, style, or text size.

3. Save the text. If you use a Mac, add *.html* to the end of the filename (for example, page.html). On a Windows machine, add *.htm* to the filename (for example, page.htm).

4. Add HTML tags to your document. Follow the example on the next page. The tags appear inside the < > signs. You must include these signs and type the tags exactly as shown, including capitalization and spacing. Proofread carefully, then save. I've added notes outside the frame to explain the function of each HTML tag.

continued ...

MATERIALS
- a computer with a modem hooked to a phone line
- an Internet service provider (a company that links you to the Internet)
- a text editor, such as SimpleText for Mac or Notepad for Windows
- a Web browser, such as Netscape Navigator or Microsoft's Internet Explorer
- free software (available online) for uploading your page

EXAMPLE

Text With HTML Tags

```
<HTML>
<HEAD>
<TITLE> Art Festival</TITLE>
</HEAD>
<BODY>
Come to the Community Arts Festival
<BR>
<BR>
See paintings, sculpture, photographs, mobiles,
puppet shows, mimes, a topiary, and much more!
<BR>
<BR>
Where? Town Hall. When? April 8, noon to dusk.
</BODY>
</HTML>
```

<HTML> tells the computer that this is a Web document.

Text between <TITLE> and </TITLE> appears in the browser's window bar when the page is viewed on the Web.

The <BODY> tag goes before the text you want to appear on your page.

The <BR> tag tells the computer to go to the next line. Use two of these tags to leave a blank line between two lines of text.

Use </BODY> to mark the end of the text on your Web page.

</HTML> tells the computer that this Web document is finished.

Finished Web Page

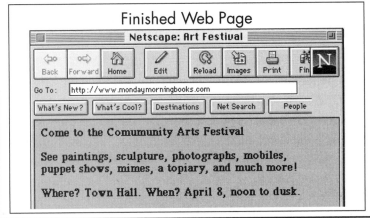

5. Open your page with your Web browser. Use the Open File or Open Local command. If you see any errors, go back to your text editor.

6. Contact your ISP (Internet service provider) to find out how to upload your file to the Web. Most ISPs will store your page on their server at no charge and will tell you (a) how to download the free software for uploading your page to their site, (b) how to upload your file, and (c) the address of your page.

7. Upload your page. It can be viewed by anyone in the world with Internet access. You'll be internationally published!

8. To revise your page, make the changes in your HTML document. Then upload it again. The new version will replace the old one.

ADDING PICTURES TO YOUR WEB PAGE

Pictures can give important information. For example, if you're writing an article about making paper airplanes, diagrams can be a big plus. The first time you add pictures to your Web page, allow a couple of hours. After practice, the job will go faster.

Do not publish copyrighted art on the Web without the owner's permission. To avoid the hassle, draw your own pictures on a computer. If you prefer to scan your own drawings or photos at home or at a copy shop, start with Step 3.

DIRECTIONS

1. Draw a graphic using your computer painting program. A graphic can be a diagram or a picture of a person, a place, a thing, or an object. The larger the graphic, the longer it takes people to view your page, so you might want to keep it small.

2. Save the graphic under the title "image."

3. Open the picture with your graphic conversion program.

4. Use the Trim or Crop command to trim the extra space around the edges of the graphic.

continued ...

MATERIALS

In addition to what you needed to make the rest of your page, you'll need:
• a computer painting program, such as KidPix
• a graphic conversion program, such as GraphicConverter for Macs and LView Pro for Windows—available as shareware on the Internet

5. If your picture has an irregular shape, delete the white area around it. Look for the Transparency tool, a wand with a small square on the end of it. Use this tool to click on the white background.

6. Using the Save As command, save your art as image.GIF. Place it in the folder or directory containing your HTML document. *GIF*, by the way, stands for "Graphic Interface Format."

7. Launch your Web browser. View the graphic by going to Open File.

8. If there's anything you want to change, go back to Step 1. If the picture looks OK, open your HTML document with your text editor and add this line immediately after the <BODY> tag:

    <IMG SRC="image.GIF">

This line tells the computer that the image source—the picture to display—is a file called "image.GIF." Save it.

9. View the HTML document with your Web browser. The image should appear just before your text. If it does, bravo! If it doesn't, don't feel bad. Remember, we said this is a tricky task. Go back through the steps, double-checking to make sure you followed them carefully. Check spelling, punctuation, and capitals in your HTML document. Make sure the filename in the IMG SRC tag you added in Step 8 matches your graphic filename perfectly. Save after making necessary changes.

10. When the page displays properly, upload it and the graphic file as you were instructed by your ISP. Note: When you upload the graphic file, you'll need to specify that it is a binary file.

Elnora Chambers has taught computer skills in schools around the world. She is the author of *The Kid-Friendly Computer Book* (Monday Morning Books).

HOW TO Make a Sports Video
—by Mark Whiteley

Watching sports on TV can be entertaining. But it's more fun to create a sports video. If you've ever wanted to make a tape to show off the sports you love, here are a few guidelines to get you started.

DIRECTIONS

1. Love and understand your subject. This is the most important factor in being able to create good-looking sports videos. If you are taping basketball, make sure you've played some hoops and watched games on TV or at a park. Study how people dribble, pass, and shoot. You must know the fundamentals before you tape them.

2. Get comfortable with the equipment. Know where the on/off record buttons are, how the batteries come on and off, and how the focus and zoom functions work. Practice looking through the viewfinder and comparing what you see with real space. It is important to be able to judge where your subject is in relation to yourself. If a ball suddenly comes flying straight at you, you're going to want to know how much time you have to duck.

3. If you want to tape action while you move, get to know your camera's weight and size. You need to sense if you're losing control of it so that you can protect the equipment. This is particularly important if you're on a skateboard or on rollerblades. I've fallen while shooting a few times in my career. It isn't fun, but I've never damaged a camera. That's partly luck, but also preparation.

continued ...

4. Focus on the essence of your sport. It could be power as in weight lifting, or grace as in ice dancing. In skateboarding—the sport I've most often shot—the essence is quick action. I show it through camera angle and framing.

• Angle: The closer the camera is to the ground, the faster the action seems. Watch a skateboarder go by while you lie on the ground and see for yourself.

• Framing: Keep it tight. Fill the frame with the subject. The background will whiz by, and the skater's actions will move your eye around the screen faster.

5. Bracket the action. Start the tape a few seconds before the action begins and stop a few seconds after it ends. You don't want to capture only half of your friend's bike jump off a high cliff. (Just kidding!)

6. Edit what you shoot. When you've got the footage you need (this often takes a while), start to piece the video together. Start by watching the footage all the way through once, and take notes. This will make it easier for you to decide what to keep and also how to order the good shots. More and more editing is done digitally on a multimedia computer. If you don't have such equipment, see the sidebar for another way to edit your material.

Remember, everything takes practice, especially when you are dealing with special equipment like cameras and VCRs. Good luck!

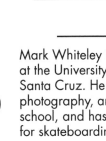

VIDEO EDITING TIPS

Professional editing equipment is expensive, but you can make an entertaining tape with only your camera, VCR, and a set of audio/visual cables.

• Plug the cables from the camera's A/V output plugs to the VCR's A/V input plugs.

• Set the VCR channel to AV (audio/visual), which is usually located one channel down from "2" on the channel selector. Now you can watch your tape on the TV.

• Play the footage from the camera, and when you see action that you want to use, rewind to the beginning of that section and start recording with the VCR.

• After editing the footage, you can add music by recording onto another tape.

Mark Whiteley is an art major at the University of California at Santa Cruz. He began videotaping, photography, and film work in high school, and has worked professionally for skateboarding companies and magazines.

HOW TO Write FICTION

—by James Morrow

I have a great job. My editors expect me to spend several hours each day putting nonexistent people through imaginary adventures. It's like getting paid for dreaming.

Most of the novels and stories I write are labeled "science fiction." However, the following principles apply to all types of fiction, from stories set in your own backyard to stories set on the back of the moon.

DIRECTIONS

1. Write about what you don't know. Trust your imagination. Too often the beginner hears: "Write about what you know." (I can't speak for you, but if my life were made into a movie, I wouldn't go to see it.) A much more useful rule: "Write about what you can fool people into believing you know."

You don't need to have lived through a shipwreck, or a tornado, before treating such subjects in fiction. But you must do the research—reading nonfiction books, talking to informants—that will enable you to lie convincingly about the matter at hand. This principle applies even with the wildest fantasy. If your main character is a dragon, don't settle for an off-the-shelf dragon. Base the dragon on your Uncle Leon.

Trick of the trade: First write the story, then do the research. If you're going full blast on a fable about a penguin who learns to fly, and suddenly you need to specify an Antarctic sea, write "Lake Michigan" and keep on going.

continued ...

It was a freezing cold day in Siberia...

2. Be nice to your mother but mean to your hero.

The difference between life and fiction is that fiction has a plot. In most well-plotted stories, the main character wants something, badly—the mining rights on Ganymede, a game-winning home run, a math teacher's approval—but some obstacle stands in the way. When the character encounters the obstacle, conflict results.

Fiction feeds on conflict. Without the Big Bad Wolf, "The Three Little Pigs" is just a catalogue of building materials. When I've finished a story or novel, I can always point to one particular element and say, "That's my obstacle. That's my Big Bad Wolf." The "wolf" might be another character (a tyrant, a little brother), a force of nature (a storm, a disease), or even a flaw in the hero.

Trick of the trade: If you're being insufficiently mean to your hero, the classic "playwright's formula" can sometimes help. In Act One, put the hero up a tree; in Act Two, throw rocks at him; in Act Three, get him out of the tree...or let him fall.

James Morrow has received the Nebula Award, given by the Science Fiction Writers of America, for "The Deluge" (voted Best Short Story of 1988) and for *City of Truth* (voted Best Novella of 1992). His Web site is: http://www.sff.net/people/Jim.Morrow.

3. A word is worth a thousand pictures.

When producing the first several drafts of a story or chapter, I usually concentrate on getting the plot to work. Then the fun begins: rewriting each sentence until the reader starts to experience the scene. With drafts three, four, and five, my energy goes into finding the exact words—sometimes the exact word—that will make a given character, object, action, or setting come alive.

• *early draft:* She was self-confident.
• *later draft:* She could prosecute honey before a jury of bears and win.

Trick of the trade: Post the names of the five senses in your work area. Your task is to make the reader see, hear, smell, taste, and feel.

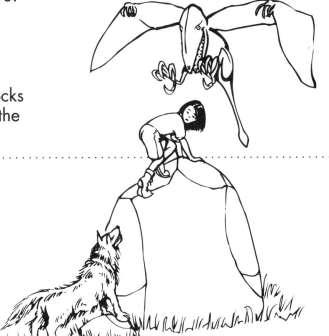

HOW TO Do Voice-Overs

—by April Winchell

I performed in my first cartoon when I was eleven years old. I had never done any voice work before, I didn't have any training, and I wasn't even all that good at it. But I had one important thing going for me: I was a good listener.

Now that may sound funny considering we're talking about a business in which you're doing all the talking. But it's only by being a great listener that you become a great voice actor.

When I was small, my parents gave me lots of records. But not music records. They gave me recordings of people speaking: comedy albums, old-time radio shows, radio theater, people reading poetry, and so on. I think they wanted me to watch less television and discover the joys of imagination. I would lie on the floor and close my eyes, trying to picture what the people who were speaking looked like and what they were doing.

I never got tired of this game. Since I listened to these recordings so much, I started to memorize them. I realized that everyone had a different speaking rhythm. Some were slow, some talked very fast. Some had foreign accents. I learned to imitate the voices pretty well.

But there was more to it than doing imitations. I had to learn how to free myself up and let all kinds of sounds come out of my mouth. At first I was a little self-conscious, because a lot of the things I tried weren't very good. But I learned that the sounds you make don't always have to be good. In fact, you can expect the first voices you create to be less interesting because they're easy. The deeper you dig and the more you let your imagination run wild, the more creative you'll become.

Here's how to explore your own voice talent. Who knows? You just might surprise yourself.

DIRECTIONS

1. Listen to spoken-word recordings. Check out books on tape at the library. Watch cartoons with your eyes closed. Look for old-time radio shows on public radio stations. Start learning to appreciate the music and rhythm of the spoken word. Take note of voices you particularly enjoy, or characterizations that make you laugh.

2. Imitate. It doesn't matter if your imitations aren't exactly dead-on. In fact, it's better if they're not. The important thing is to develop a good ear. When I created Tanya on "The Mighty Ducks" animated series, I did a female version of Woody Allen, only with a cold. Of course, nobody would think in a million years that Tanya sounds like Woody Allen, and she shouldn't! It was the vocal quality that gave me the idea; I built from there.

3. Work with a tape recorder. Try doing every voice you can think of (including your own) into a tape recorder. Then play it back.

Interesting, isn't it? Your voice doesn't sound anything like it does in your head. That's because you hear your own voice from a completely different perspective. When you speak, you actually hear your voice resonating through your sinuses, your skull, even your ear bones. It took me years to get used to the sound of my own voice. But it's a very important thing to do. You have to learn to think of your voice as someone else's, so that you can be objective about your performance.

continued ...

As our bathosphere sinks to the ocean floor...

4. Work with comic books or magazines.
Almost every time I do a cartoon, the director gives me a drawing of the character I'm going to play. It tells me a lot about what the character should sound like. How old is the character? Younger people have higher voices. How is the character's mouth shaped? An overbite might cause the character to lisp. Try taking a comic book into the bathroom and standing in front of the mirror with it. Make your mouth or facial expression similar to the character's in the book. What do you sound like?

5. Make a list of your voices.
Every time you come up with a voice, give it a name and put it on paper. This is important for a couple of reasons. First, it shows you how much progress you're making. And second, it keeps you from forgetting what you've come up with! When I first started in this business, I kept my list with me all the time. When a director asked me to try a couple of different voices, I sometimes got nervous and went blank. With my list handy, I could think on my feet much faster.

6. Read aloud.
Never miss an opportunity to read aloud. If your teacher asks for volunteers, be one of them. After all, voice work is really all about reading out loud. The more you practice, the better you'll be.

7. Most important—have fun!
Like any creative art, voice work is better when you're having fun. It's such a creative, spontaneous, playful way to make a living. Concentrate on what you do well and enjoy doing, because that will allow you to create from a place of joy. People always know when you're doing something because you love it. They can see and feel your happiness in your work. And that's the key to success in any endeavor.

The Wolf is coming! The Wolf is coming!

April Winchell has worked on hundreds of film and television projects such as *101 Dalmatians, Who Framed Roger Rabbit,* and *Casper.* Cartoons are a family business; her father, Paul Winchell, was the voice of Tigger. April runs her own radio production company in Los Angeles.

HOW TO Practice Music

—by Judith Shatin

Playing an instrument is like dancing. To learn your instrument, you need to practice your moves, just like for ballet or basketball.

DIRECTIONS

1. Find a quiet place. It should be available for at least one half hour, five days a week. Look for a room where your practice won't disturb others.

2. Warm up for several minutes playing exercises. These simple pieces teach you the moves you need for more complex compositions. If your instrument permits, work on scales. When bored, stop! Move around. Take a break. Sing the pattern. Then try again.

3. Learn a piece from a score.
• If you like, listen to a recording ahead of time.
• Now play the piece slowly. This is called sight reading.
• Next, break the piece into short chunks (phrases), and repeat them until you can play them easily. Don't rush. If you're making many errors, you're playing too fast.
• Practice the composition as a whole. If you have questions about what you're doing, keep notes that you can share with your teacher.
• Memorize the piece. Again, build up phrase by phrase. Memorizing will help you learn to think in music, just as you think in words.

4. Create your own music. Imitate music you like, or make up something else. You can record it or write it down. You are on your way to becoming a musician.

LEARNING BY EAR
Take any melody, sing it, and then try playing it on your instrument. If you have trouble with any spots, sing them or listen to a recording and practice those spots slowly. Play at least one new tune a week this way.

Judith Shatin is chair, McIntire Department of Music, at the University of Virginia. She is also director of the Virginia Center for Computer Music.

HOW TO Take Travel Photographs

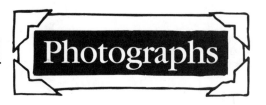

—by Michael Stinson

There's nothing mysterious about taking exciting, attention-getting travel photographs. Of course, you need a camera and film. But the main ingredient is a keen eye for the visual elements that go into a dynamic photograph.

DIRECTIONS

1. Get a camera. Photographic cameras come in all shapes and sizes. A simple 35mm "point and shoot" camera is fine for grab shots that allow little time for adjusting focus and exposure. But the best choice for travel photography is a 35mm SLR (single-lens-reflect) camera. Most camera manufacturers produce models in a variety of price ranges. The most basic of these is perfectly adequate for taking travel photographs.

2. Get several lenses. One advantage of the 35mm SLR camera is that you can switch lenses. These cameras come with a 50mm lens as standard equipment. This type of lens perceives the world in a manner similar to the human eye. For travel photography, two additional lenses are very helpful:
• a wide-angle lens (typically 35mm), which has a wider field of view
• a telephoto lens (typically 70mm), which has a longer field of view
Another option is a zoom lens, which incorporates a range of focal lengths; in a sense, it's a combination lens—wide, standard, and telephoto all in one.

continued ...

3. Choose your film. If you're a beginner, start with color print or transparency film in the ASA/ISO 64 - 100 range. As you gain experience, consider these three issues when you buy film:

• *Color vs. black and white*: Most travel photographers prefer color, but in some situations black-and-white shots are more dramatic.

• *Speed*: You can buy film in a range of speeds, from very fast (ASA/ISO 3200) to very slow (ASA/ISO 25). Fast film works well in low-light situations without a flash, but tends to be grainy. Slow film is very sharp but requires strong light.

• *Print or transparency*: Print film is for paper photographs that you can store in an album. Transparency film is used to make slides that can be projected onto a screen. In general, print film is more practical because it is cheaper and easier to work with. However, for special occasions, such as publishing in magazines, transparency film is better because it offers more brilliant and dramatic color.

4. Know the basic techniques. If you want to create interesting and memorable travel photographs, think about the following three issues:

• *Composition*: Learn the "law of thirds." The most important element should <u>not</u> be placed in the center of the frame but in the outer third (upper or lower, right or left). This makes a photo seem more dynamic.

• *Depth of field*: Experiment with your aperture ring to control how much of the scene is in focus. Under the right conditions, you can have the subject in focus— for example, a statue—and things closer to the camera and farther away blurry. This technique takes practice, but the results can be dramatic.

• *Color*: Keep an eye out for dramatic color accents. For very bright, sunny days consider using a polarizing filter (which screws directly over the lens) to cut glare and increase color intensity.

DO'S AND DON'TS

• Do study great photographs in magazines, such as *National Geographic* or in the collected works of photographic geniuses, such as Ansel Adams and Henri Cartier-Bresson.

• Do use your wide-angle lens for landscapes and interiors. It has excellent depth of field and the ability to expand space.

• Do use your telephoto lens for portraits and candid shots. It produces a flattering look by compressing distance and "flattening" the subject.

• Do use your standard lens for low-light photography. It generally offers the largest possible aperture.

• Don't be afraid to photograph strangers. People are often the most interesting subjects for travel photography. Taking candid photos, where people look natural, is tricky. It's courteous to ask people if you can photograph them, but often the result will be a stilted-looking shot. An alternative is to use a telephoto lens so that the subject isn't aware that you're shooting.

• Don't go out without your camera. The best travel photographs happen when you least expect them.

• Don't keep your camera stuffed inside a case with the cap on. By the time you get to it, your perfect travel photograph may be history.

• Do keep your negatives or transparencies organized in plastic "sleeves" that protect the film and make it easier to locate specific images for printing. For prints, a folio-size book with stiff pages is a great way to mount and display your work.

• Don't keep bad photographs. Shots that are out of focus, poorly composed, or under- or over-exposed belong in one place only: the round file (waste basket). Top photographers keep only one shot out of ten.

Michael Stinson wandered the globe from 1982 to 1992 as a travel photojournalist. He now lives in Los Angeles and writes for the movies.

HOW TO Speak a Poem Aloud

—by John Felstiner

Speaking a poem is like performing a piece of music.

DIRECTIONS

1. Choose a short poem that you like. It can be any sort of poem that matters to you and that takes you somewhere new.

2. Read the poem many times silently. Read it until its lines become familiar and each phrase seems right. If you don't understand a word, look it up. Then continue reading. You might even memorize the poem, all to the good when presenting it.

3. Read aloud, alone or to someone. Begin by speaking the poem's title. Sense the rhythm of the lines and the physical sound of the words, and which words and syllables want a strong emphasis.

4. Vary your delivery. Decide where to speak slowly or fast, and where to raise or lower the pitch of your voice. Before or after a telling moment, try an extra long pause.

5. Pronounce words crisply. Don't drop your voice too much at the end of a line or sentence. You can pause for a fraction of a second at the end of a line even if its sense runs on to the next line. You may need to speak slower and louder than usual, but keep your natural expressiveness.

6. Relate to the audience. Make eye contact, gesture to bring out something dramatic, and move around a bit.

Tyger, tyger, burning bright...

Whose woods these are I think I know...

Once upon a midnight dreary...

John Felstiner teaches literature at Stanford University. He has written books on Max Beerbohm and Pablo Neruda. His biography *Paul Celan: Poet, Survivor, Jew* won the 1997 Truman Capote Award for Literary Criticism.

HOW TO Be a Stand-up Comedian
—by Steve Silberberg

Performing stand-up comedy is fun. But just because you like to laugh doesn't mean you can make other people laugh. If you don't have a sense of humor, you can't develop one by attending a comedy class or reading a book. Some people claim they can teach you how to be funny. They're lying. It's not like baking a cake. YOU CAN'T LEARN HOW TO DO COMEDY JUST BY READING A LIST OF DIRECTIONS!

LIST OF DIRECTIONS

1. Don't steal material. You don't learn to be funny by doing another comedian's routine. And you'll know deep down that they're laughing at someone else's jokes, not yours.

2. Record every funny idea that you have. Since you never know when a funny thought will occur, always carry a tape recorder or notebook. People will think you're strange if you do this while talking to them. But the fact is: comedians *are* strange.

3. Write your schtick. Your "schtick" is your act, your routine—all the funny "bits" you say and do during your time on stage. Unless you're an impersonator, do not copy someone else's style.

4. Be concise. Most new comics write jokes that are too long. If you omit a phrase, does the joke still work? It probably works even better. You may need to rewrite a "bit" many times to get it right.

continued ...

5. Don't be afraid to bomb. You will. The real failure is NOT performing. You're absolutely guaranteed to get no laughs if you don't perform.

6. Sign up for an "Open Mike" night at a local comedy club. Open Mikes are designed for comedians to test their acts and try out new material. The first time you perform, you'll need about five minutes of original material. If you're new, expect to go on stage last. This is called "paying your dues."

7. Perform for unbiased audiences. When your friends come to see you, they'll pretend to laugh.

8. Tape your act. Some people wrongly think that every joke they do is gold. Tapes can help you identify the parts of your act that need improvement.

9. Perform frequently. This is the single best way to improve. Experience gives you unshakable nerves, confidence, and swagger: all needed for doing quality stand-up.

10. Keep writing new material. There's nothing more boring than doing the same act over and over. People will be angry they wasted money to see you rehash the "bit" about your wacky aunt.

11. Speak your truth. Listen to the inner voice that moves you. If you do, you are likely to succeed.

12. Understand your desire to make people laugh. While this will not help you be funny, at least you'll remember why you drove 19 hours to bomb in front of eight people for 100 dollars.

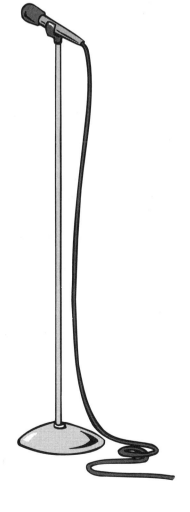

WORKING THE CROWD

You can show off your brilliant wit by bantering with the audience. This makes people feel part of the show. Your clever off-the-cuff remarks prove that you're more than a talking chimp reciting old jokes. "Working the crowd" is what makes a live act different from what's on TV.

WRITING A ROUTINE

Here's the classic formula for writing a bit:

- Choose a *topic* that interests you, say, whales.
- Think up a *premise*. This is your starting point, for example, you're an environmentalist.
- Think up the *twist*. A twist is your clever insight, for example, you're an environmentalist who went whaling.
- Write your *set-up*. This is how your "bit" will begin on stage: "You know, I'm an environmentalist, but the other day I did something utterly reprehensible. I went whaling."
- Add the *punch line*. Here's where you get your big laugh. "What a waste of time! I couldn't get the plankton on the hook!"

Now consider what this example taught you about stand-up comedy. Exactly. It taught you that I'm a stupid moron. Supposedly, you learned that bits need a premise, a set-up, a twist, and a punch line. Ultimately, you learned a formula. But watch out! Although this formula is the most common way of structuring a bit these days, don't let it box you in and limit your creativity. If you have a different way of making people laugh, do it. Don't alter your style to conform to some established method.

In the 1930s, a pie in the face was considered the height of humor. No premise, no set-up, no twist. All punch line. A bit needs one thing and one thing only. **A funny punch line**. That's it. The secret is out.

But make sure the punch line is the last thing you say (or do). That seems obvious, but many comedians continue to ramble on and on long after the point has been made, and bore the audience, as I'm illustrating right now.

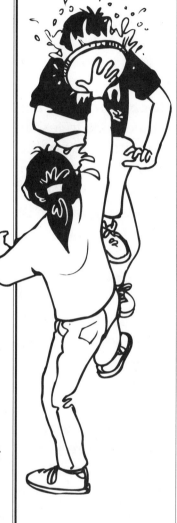

Steve Silberberg is a professional comedian with an MS from MIT and a huge ego. He has worked as a software contractor, comedy writer, college professor, and film producer. He is also a cartoonist, an aerobics instructor, an Internet geek, an air sickness bag collector, and a museum curator.

PART 2

DAILY
LIFE

HOW TO Be Street Aware and Safe
—by Al Johnson

A crime can happen to you anywhere, at any time. Your best defense is to notice what is happening around you. Keep your eyes open. Be alert. The following suggestions are meant to help you get to your destination safely. Discuss them with your family and friends.

DIRECTIONS

1. Before you leave home, tell someone where you're going and when you'll return. This person should know what you're wearing.

2. Be aware of your surroundings. Where are the open fields and empty buildings? Are there cars parked on your street that usually aren't there?

3. Pay attention to people. Notice where they are and what they are doing. Is a suspicious-looking person driving around your neighborhood?

4. If possible, walk with a buddy or a group. If you must walk alone, walk faster than you think you need to. Walk facing traffic so you can see approaching cars and be prepared if someone stops. Once in a while, look behind you to see if someone is following you.

5. If someone is following you, go quickly to the nearest place where you can find people. Try a restaurant, a store, a post office, a gas station, etc. Explain what's happening and ask the person to help you get to where you are going safely.

continued ...

6. If someone is walking toward you and makes you feel funny, cross the street quickly. Don't slow down or confront the person. Go find help.

7. If a stranger talks to you first, don't reply. Don't talk to anyone who asks you to help find a pet. Don't believe a person who says he or she was told by your parents or a neighbor to pick you up.

8. If someone tries to take you, quickly get away and scream "Fire!" while running for help. Yelling "Fire!" gets more attention than "Help!" If you can't get away, yell, "This person is trying to hurt me!"

9. Remember details. If you have been approached by someone suspicious or were offered candy or a ride, tell your parents or the police as soon as possible. The police investigator may ask you about the person's appearance: clothing; coloring of the person's skin, hair, and eyes; if the person wore glasses or had a tattoo; and whether the person walked with a limp or carried a weapon. You will be able to make a quick and accurate description after you have had some practice observing. (See sidebar.)

Good luck and remember: being aware is the key to your safety.

OBSERVING EXERCISE

The next time you and a friend or your parents are waiting in line at the market, movies, or mall, look at a particular person in front of you. Remember as many things about that person as you can. When you get home, you and your friend should separately write down details about the person and compare the lists. Practicing this observation skill is fun and will help you better identify individuals after seeing them only for a brief time. This is something the whole family can try together.

Al Johnson is founder of The Young, Alert, and Aware Program designed to help kids avoid and escape from dangerous situations. For information write: P.O. Box 273, Redondo Beach, California 90277. Phone: (310) 792-8112. Fax: (310) 792-0095. Toll free in the U.S.: (888) 853-6748.

HOW TO Talk to a Doctor
—by Dr. Harry Hartzell

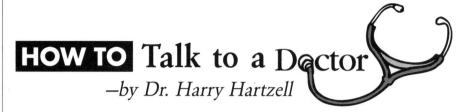

A doctor may use all sorts of tools and tests to find out what's happening with your body. However, some of the most important information can come from you if you are prepared to share your observations and concerns. Discussing body parts and functions may seem strange or embarrassing. After all, you don't do it every day. But if you learn to speak openly about these matters, you can help your doctor help you.

DIRECTIONS

1. Plan for your visit. Review exactly what is bothering you. Some patients find it helpful to describe a problem on paper ahead of time.

2. Understand that nothing you say will embarrass your doctor. Physicians spend years studying all parts and functions of the body. Matters that seldom come up in your life are part of your doctor's everyday work.

3. Do not hide information. Your doctor can't read your mind. If some part of your body hurts or if you have noticed a change, bring this to your doctor's attention. If you feel embarrassed, just say so. This will let the doctor know how you feel, and it may even help you become more comfortable.

The following analogy may be useful: If you brought a machine to a repair person, you would do all that you could to make sure the expert knew what the problem was. You need to have the same attitude when seeking medical care.

continued ...

4. If you don't know the scientific word for a body part or function, use plain language. In some cases, you can point to the place. If that doesn't work, tell the doctor, "I don't know how to say this." The doctor will help you explain the problem and may tell you the medical word for future use. Keep in mind: Your body is part of nature. Even things that may seem gross—for example, pus and scabs—relate to amazing processes that are worth understanding.

5. If you are worried about how you compare with other people, discuss this with your doctor. Common worries have to do with height, weight, skin, eyesight, hearing, reading or other skills, diet, and the shapes of body parts. Sometimes a small difference can make someone feel miserable. By sharing your concern, you may discover that there is nothing to worry about. But if there is a problem, discussing it with your doctor can be an important first step in dealing with it.

6. Answer the doctor's questions truthfully. If you don't understand a question, say so. Then the doctor can restate the question. This is much better than having you guess at what the doctor needs to know. If you want to know why a doctor asked you something or did a certain test, ask about it. This knowledge may make you more comfortable when communicating with your doctor.

7. If you have your own questions, ask them. For example, if you think that a symptom means you have a serious illness, tell the doctor what you think. Your view of your symptoms can be important to helping the doctor understand what's going on with you.

Dr. Harry Hartzell practiced pediatrics for 33 years at the Palo Alto Medical Clinic.

HOW TO Give the Perfect Gift

—by Annalisa McMorrow

Imagine receiving a present wrapped in pretty paper. You enjoy the moment of anticipation, wondering what's inside. Then you tear it open. Wow! It's just what you wanted!

The key to giving the perfect gift is capturing the feeling of happy surprise that you feel when *you* receive a wonderful present. Read on to discover how to give someone else that special feeling.

DIRECTIONS

1. Spend time brainstorming. The best gifts come from the heart, not the wallet. You don't need to spend much money when you give a present. You only need to spend your time and energy to think about the person who will be receiving the present. Does your friend have a hobby? A favorite author? A collection? A lack of time? A favorite food?

2. Create it. Once you find a theme for your gift, the gift itself can come naturally. If your friend reads a lot, you can make a special bookmark that lists books by a favorite author, or books in a certain genre (mystery, history, fiction). If your friend has a hobby, paint a T-shirt with your friend's name and a slogan that says "Greatest Baseball Player on Earth" or "Number 1 Ballerina." If your pal is always busy, make coupons for little treats that your friend can redeem at any time. You can make a coupon for dog walking, car washing, baby sitting. (These are great gifts for your parents, too.) If your friend is a cookie fiend, bake a batch of homemade chocolate chip cookies. Or invite your pal to a special birthday dinner, cooked by you.

continued ...

3. Find it for cheap. If you do buy a gift, make sure that it's extra-special. This doesn't mean breaking your piggy bank. It means thinking about what your friend really likes. If your pal has a special collection (marbles, Pez dispensers, cookie cutters, stamps, models) you can keep an eye open all the time. Look at garage sales, flea markets, thrift stores, and so on. Whenever you see something your friend might like, buy it. Then keep the gift to give for a special occasion: your friend's birthday, Valentine's Day, or just as a surprise.

4. Make the gift count. If you would rather buy a gift than make one, consider the fact that gifts can include events, rather than things. Get tickets to the circus, or to a concert of your friend's favorite band. Or give a gift that lasts 12 months by buying your pal a subscription to a magazine featuring something he or she likes (like race cars, or wildlife, or monster movies). Every month, your friend will think of you when the mail comes!

You may have heard the saying "It's better to give than it is to receive." When you give the perfect gift, the smile on your friend's face will make that saying come true!

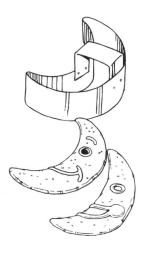

GIFT IDEAS FOR SPECIAL OCCASIONS

Going Away Gifts: Make a huge card and have your pals sign it.

Valentine's Day Gifts: Cut a photo of the two of you into a heart shape and glue it to a doily.

Birthday Bonanzas: Make an audiotape of all your friends singing "Happy Birthday."

Earth-smart Gifts: Instead of buying cut flowers, plant a window box or an herb garden.

New Home Gifts: Have a photograph of your pal's friends blown up to poster size to decorate his or her new room.

Cooperative Gifts (or April Fool's Day Gifts): Get together with a group of pals and have each person write down a joke. Bind the pages together to make a joke book.

Annalisa McMorrow is a free-lance writer. She has written many film and concert reviews. Her books include a science series for early childhood education. She gives approximately 50 gifts a year.

HOW TO Do a Manicure

—by Kimberly Shumate

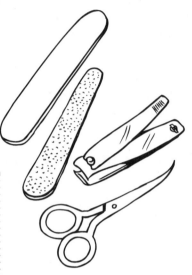

Clean, well-groomed hands make a silent statement about you. They reveal your attention to detail. It doesn't matter whether you're male or female. It doesn't matter what you do. I've given manicures to all sorts of people, including teachers, actors, business leaders, musicians, and doctors. Whoever you are, others will notice your hands and nails. That's why you should take time to pamper yourself with a manicure. It's not hard to do, and can even be fun.

DIRECTIONS

1. Get an emery board. Never use a metal file. An emery board is gentler on nail surfaces and will minimize cracking and splitting.

2. File in one direction. Scrubbing back and forth is harmful to the strength of the nail, so be kind.

3. To shape your nail, follow the line at the base of your nail bed. The nail bed is the pink area. The overall shape should be square or oval, never pointed. Always leave the sides of the nail intact.

4. Keep the length less than half the nail bed length. Of course, some jobs require a shorter length. Most men will want to clip nails approximately 1/16 to 1/8 of an inch (1.5 mm to 3 mm) from the free edge.

continued ...

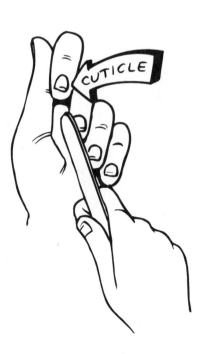

CUTICLE

5. Apply lotion. Lotion and cuticle oil on the hands are like water in the desert. They overcome dryness and promote healing. Massage any moisturizer into the cuticle area and wait five minutes. For an extra treat, especially in the winter, apply lotion, then cover with lightweight cotton gloves or socks and sleep through the night. In the morning, you will find softer, smoother hands.

6. Polish the nails. Before starting, set up an area in a well-ventilated room. Cover the work surface.
- Use polish only in a well-ventilated room.
- For long-lasting results, make the nail surface as clean and dry as possible. Use soap and water, then polish remover. Avoid touching your cuticle with the remover.
- Always use a base and top coat. The base coat will prepare the nail and help the polish adhere; the top coat will seal the polish for longer wear.
- Use two coats of nail color. Be sure to cover the tip of the nail. Note: It is very important not to touch the cuticle with polish because it will dry the skin. To avoid this, point your fingertip downward so the polish will slide away from your skin.
- Dry the polish by dipping nails in cold water for two or three minutes. Bottled nail dryers are made from oil, which makes nails slippery but not dry.

SPECIAL PROBLEMS

Cuticles: The cuticle is a delicate piece of skin. The correct treatment for cuticles is never to cut them but instead to apply a healthy amount of oil on the area and gently push them back using an orange wood stick or a Q-tip. For everyday maintenance, push cuticles back with a hand towel when hands are wet.

Hangnails: A hangnail isn't a nail, but a piece of skin pulled away from the finger. Causes include excessive hand-washing, handling of paper products, and cold weather. When you have a hangnail, don't pull it. Don't nibble it. Clip! That's what nippers are for. Press the lower edge of the blade against the base of the hangnail and close carefully but forcefully.

Kimberly Shumate has been a manicurist since 1980 and holds four state licenses. She has worked on advertisements, movie and television sets, and magazine covers. Clients include Elton John and Eric Roberts.

HOW TO Prevent Home Accidents

—adapted from Peterborough County-City Health Unit materials

Many accidents are predictable and preventable. By going on a "hazard hunt," you can make your home safer for those who live and visit there. Although no environment is entirely risk free, much can be done to reduce the risk of injury. Help your family become safety-conscious with the tips below.

DIRECTIONS

1. Falls. Danger areas include stairways, slippery floors, windows, trees, roofs, and sidewalks.
• Always pick up objects that might trip people, such as toys, tools, and fallen branches.
• Immediately wipe spills and wet floors in the kitchen, the bathroom, and elsewhere.
• Use a sturdy ladder to reach high things. Have a second person hold the ladder.
• Use a non-skid mat in the shower.
• Clear snow, ice, and wet leaves from walkways.
• Repair or get rid of rickety or unstable furniture.

2. Drowning.
• Don't go swimming alone.
• Never leave an infant alone, even for a few seconds, in a bath, pool, or other body of water.

3. Suffocating. If small children are present, remove plastic bags, small toys, uninflated balloons, and other objects that can be swallowed.

continued …

CAUTION!
Because accident prevention involves risks—for example, dealing with unknown chemicals—this project should be done only with adult involvement.

4. Fires and burns.
- Install smoke alarms. Change batteries yearly, or when needed.
- Develop a fire escape plan. It should include two escape routes from each location, plus an outside meeting place. Hold fire drills, including practice sessions in the dark.
- Make sure pot handles are turned inward on the stove.
- Put bulbs of correct size and wattage in fixtures.
- Don't plug many appliances into one cord or outlet. Replace frayed cords.
- Keep a working fire extinguisher to handle small fires, especially in the kitchen.
- Keep electrical appliances away from water.
- Use plug blocks if young children are in the home.

5. Natural disasters.
Develop plans to deal with earthquakes, tornadoes, hurricanes, floods, or other happenings that occur in your area. Contact your fire department or emergency preparedness organization for information.

6. Poisonings.
Not all poisons are obvious. Perfumes, lotions, cosmetics, alcohol, paints, sealers, and thinners can be toxic.
- Keep all dangerous materials in their original containers. Don't remove warning labels.
- Never store any solution in an unmarked bottle. If you find an unknown liquid, contact your sanitation department for disposal instructions.
- Store cleaning supplies separately from foods.
- Keep potentially dangerous materials—including vitamins and medicines—in high cabinets with safety latches, out of the reach of infants.

Contact your local emergency preparedness organization for more information. Also, because even the best accident-prevention plan cannot prevent all accidents, it makes sense to:
- Take a first aid course.
- Post emergency telephone numbers.

Peterborough County-City Health Unit is located in Ontario, Canada. These materials were co-developed by the Kiwanis Club of Peterborough.

The Day I Saved a Life
—by Blanca Vargas

As part of our high school science program, my teacher, Ms. Hansen Guzman, invited Sequoia Hospital to provide a teacher so students might earn a CPR certificate. CPR stands for "cardiopulmonary resuscitation," a method for helping people who are having a medical crisis.

For three days, we were taught resuscitation (reviving someone who's unconscious) and also the Heimlich maneuver (an emergency technique for removing something blocking the windpipe). We used mannequins (infants, children, and adults) to practice. I was particularly interested as my mother suffers from diabetes. We learned how to give artificial respiration, check the patient's pulse, and clear the respiratory channels. At the end of the course, I received my certificate plus a special prize from the hospital training staff.

Four days later, I was at home with my family. We were sewing, and my nephews were eating a snack of sunflower seeds. All of a sudden Jesus, who is 16 months old, was trying to cough, turned bright red, and held his hands to his neck. My sister-in-law tried to give him water. I said, "No, let me do it." Jesus was choking and I had just learned what to do. I checked his mouth but could not see any obstruction, so I picked up the baby, put him over my left arm, and with my right hand, hit the back of his shoulder five times. By the fifth blow, the seed and a lot of saliva popped out of his mouth. He took a deep breath and started to cry. His mother hugged him. Everyone clapped hands and fussed over me.

On Monday morning, arriving in class, I told my teacher what had happened over the weekend. Then the fussing really started: local newspapermen, TV, Ms. Figone from Sequoia Hospital, the school principal, even an announcement over the school public address system, everyone complimenting me for having saved a life. My picture with Jesus and the story appeared in the newspapers and on TV.

Saving my little nephew's life gave me a very warm, happy feeling that I will never forget. This little boy will always be my favorite person.

Blanca Vargas lives in Redwood City, California, and attends Sequoia High School.

HOW TO Fix Things

—by Scott McMorrow

"If it isn't broken, don't fix it." But what happens when something *isn't* working? If you don't know what you're doing, you can make the situation worse. The tips below may help you avoid that pitfall while getting things back in working order.

DIRECTIONS

1. Compare. Look at an item that works and is identical to the one you're trying to fix. Note how the working item operates and carefully observe what the broken item is doing. This will help you identify what is wrong with the damaged object, and will show exactly what needs to be fixed.

2. Read all about it. Most items come with owner's manuals that cover trouble-shooting. If you don't have a manual, or it doesn't give enough information, look for books in the library. Chances are that someone, somewhere, has written about the item you're having trouble with. The trick is finding this material. Another place to look for information is on the World Wide Web.

3. Be creative. Picture in your mind the item's correct function and look at the broken object. Try to figure out what is wrong by remembering how it used to work. Draw pictures of the working item's function if it helps you to recall how it worked.

Fixing things can be both fun and frustrating. With clear thinking and patience you can feel the excitement of turning a broken object into a working item. Remember: if you need help, ask someone.

BE SAFE!

Make sure that you won't get hurt, harm others, or damage property while making a repair. If performing the fix might be dangerous, call in a professional. Potentially dangerous items to fix include things that run on electricity or natural gas.

Scott McMorrow is an engineer, playwright, and graphic artist.

HOW TO Clean Green

—by Annie Berthold-Bond

Old-fashioned folk cleaning recipes work! That's because they are based on good science. Unlike modern products made of synthetic chemicals, the old recipes consist of natural materials found in most kitchen cupboards. Using just five basic ingredients from old-fashioned formulas, you can clean anything in your house in a way that is less toxic, more environmentally safe, and a lot cheaper than using commercial products. Give it a try!

Note: Before using a solution in a visible area, test it in a place that is less likely to be noticed.

DIRECTIONS

1. Baking Soda. This mildly abrasive alkaline mineral has many uses for cleaning and can replace scouring powders. It absorbs odors out of the air and can replace air fresheners; it will even take smells out of clothes if added to the laundry! If water is added to it and it is left to sit on the bottom of the oven or in a greasy, crusted pan, baking soda will loosen grime better than anything else. It is even gentle enough to use on fiberglass.

• *Baking Soda Soft Scrubber*
1/2 cup (.125 liters) baking soda, enough liquid soap or detergent to make a texture like frosting

Place the baking soda in a bowl and stir in liquid soap. Scoop the mixture onto a sponge, wash the item's surface, and rinse.

• *Baking Soda Carpet Deodorizer*
Box of baking soda

Sprinkle baking soda generously over the affected area or the entire rug. Let sit overnight, then vacuum. Throw away the vacuum bag. *continued ...*

CAUTION!

• Because this activity involves chemicals, the project should be done only with adult involvement.

• When you make your own cleaning formulas, make sure to label the bottle or jar, and only mix the ingredients used in the directions.

• Ammonia and bleach are never used in these formulas—you don't need them—and you can get into trouble mixing them with the other ingredients.

2. Tea Tree Oil or Vinegar Disinfectants.

While not registered with the Environmental Protection Agency as disinfectants, tea tree oil and vinegar remove mold in the bathroom and mildew on walls. Tea tree oil is found in health food stores; vinegar is found in supermarkets.

• *Tea Tree Oil Mold Spray*
2 teaspoons (10 milliliters) tea tree oil, 2 cups (.5 liters) water, spray bottle

Pour ingredients into a spray bottle and spray. Do not rinse, but let the tea tree oil dissipate on its own (it takes a few days).

• *Vim and Vinegar*
1 cup (.25 liters) white vinegar, 1 cup water, spray bottle

Follow directions for Tea Tree Oil Mold Spray.

3. White Vinegar and Lemon Juice.

White vinegar and lemon juice are acids that can neutralize and dissolve minerals and even some dirt. Vinegar seems to draw the dirt right out of wood. Acids eat tarnish right off brass and other metals and can even kill bacteria.

• *Faucet and Fixture Fix-Up*
1/4 cup (.06 liters) vinegar, 3/4 cup (.2 liters) water

Pour the water and vinegar into a spray bottle. Shake. Spray the area and wipe with a clean cotton rag.

• *Light and Lemony Duster*
3 tablespoons (45 milliliters) lemon juice, a drop or two of vegetable oil

Mix the juice and oil in a jar. Dip a soft cotton cloth into the jar and use as a dusting cloth.

continued ...

4. Liquid Soaps and Detergents.

Soaps and detergents are used for getting grease and dirt off dishes, windows, floors, etc. If you have few minerals in your water (soft water), you can use a real soap, but if you have a lot of minerals in your water (hard water), you need a detergent because detergents are formulated so that no scum forms from the cleaning agent reacting with minerals in the water. Detergents are poisonous and should not be poured into lakes and streams because they are very toxic to fish. When you buy liquid soaps or detergents, buy those without perfumes or dyes. Health food stores have a wide variety of good products.

• *Carpet Cleaning Foam*
1/4 cup (.06 liters) liquid detergent, 3 tablespoons (45 milliliters) water

Whip ingredients in a bowl with an egg beater. Rub the foam into problem areas of rug. Rinse well.

• *All-Purpose Floor Cleaner*
1/4 cup (.06 liters) liquid detergent, 1/2 cup (.125 liters) vinegar, 2 gallons (8 liters) warm water

Pour detergent, vinegar, and water into a bucket. Swish the ingredients around to blend, and then wash the floor as you normally would.

5. Washing Soda.

A chemical neighbor of baking soda, washing soda is stronger and meant for tougher jobs. Although it releases no harmful fumes, it is very alkaline and can burn skin, so wear rubber gloves when using it. Washing soda cuts grease, cleans petroleum oils and dirt, removes wax and lipstick, and softens water. Like baking soda, it takes odors out of laundry and the air, but don't use it on fiberglass!

• *Tough Job Paste*
1/2 cup (.125 liters) washing soda, enough water to make a paste

In a bowl, add the washing soda and water. Scoop the paste onto a sponge and scrub the area to be cleaned. Let the paste rest for a while, adding water as necessary if it dries out. Rinse.

• *Heavy Duty Cleaner*
1 cup (.25 liters) washing soda, 1 gallon (4 liters) hot water

Dissolve the washing soda in a bucket by adding the hot water. Wash the area with a scrub brush or sponge. If the area is very dirty, let the mixture set for a while before rinsing. (Note: Because washing soda removes wax, don't use it on a waxed floor unless you want to remove the wax!)

Annie Berthold-Bond is the author of *Clean & Green, The Green Kitchen Handbook,* and the cleaning chapter in *The Healthy School Handbook.*

HOW TO Negotiate
—by Bert Fields

We often want something from other people. Maybe it's help on a project, or perhaps we want to borrow an item. Unfortunately, in many cases, the other person may not want to give us what we want. Can we change the person's mind? Not always. But often, getting what we want depends on how we ask for it. This is called "negotiating." Here's how to do it effectively.

DIRECTIONS

1. Offer the other person something of value. Successful negotiating requires a fair trade. Both sides must feel that they are winners. For example, before you ask to borrow a friend's tuba, figure out what your friend might like from you. It doesn't have to be the same sort of thing. You might propose to fix your friend's model airplane, or teach him or her a skill.

2. Explain why your request is important. If you just say, "I want this," the other person can easily turn you down. But it's harder for someone to say *no* when you give good reasons.

Suppose you want to borrow a friend's bike. If you explain that you need it to visit your cousin in the hospital, you improve your chance of getting a *yes*.

3. Ask again. What if the person you're negotiating with turns you down even after you offered a good trade, and even after you explained your reasons? You can always point out that there may come a time when he or she will want something from you. Then ask the person to reconsider.

4. Know when to quit asking. Sometimes the person you're negotiating with won't make a deal. This happens. Just as in sports, you won't be successful every time. You might feel disappointed. But it doesn't make a lot of sense to get angry at the other person. You must realize that the other person has a right to deny your request, just as you have the same right when someone else asks you for a favor.

Bert Fields is a well-known Hollywood lawyer.

HOW TO Invest in the Stock Market
—by Richard Chadwell

Start investing in the stock market now. Many people start this financial adventure late in life. If you begin now, you'll be ahead of the crowd! Getting involved in the market has benefits beyond making money. It increases your knowledge of economics, current events, and history.

Because it's a complex activity, there is no one right way to do it. I'll share my strategies. But you should study other investors' ideas and learn all you can about the market. If you're not familiar with some of the basic terms and ideas, you might read the "Questions and Answers About Stocks" section before trying the steps below.

DIRECTIONS

1. Set aside money to invest. If you don't have money to invest now, learn about the market by investing an imaginary sum.

2. Decide how much risk you'll take. Every investment involves risk because we can't predict the future.

But some stocks are riskier than others. "Speculative" stocks can make you great sums of money or become worthless. I recommend that beginners start with less risky companies that have a good track record for making a profit.

3. Invest for the long term. You can hold a quality stock for years and watch its worth increase.

4. Study a company before investing in it. Gather facts about its profits, products, workers, management, and competitors.

5. Go for growth. Look at a company's five-year earnings record. Purchase stocks with a proven record of increasing their earnings each year.

6. Consider investing in a company whose products you like. Each time you buy its product, you share the company's success.

7. Invest regularly. Over the years, stocks have given investors greater returns than any other investment.

8. Track your stocks at regular intervals to see how they're doing.

QUESTIONS & ANSWERS ABOUT STOCKS

The following questions and answers may help you decide whether to participate in the stock market.

What is stock? Stock is the ownership of a company, and is divided into shares. For example, if the total stock of a company is worth a million dollars, and if there are 100,000 shares of that stock, each share is worth 10 dollars. When you buy shares of a company's stock, you are a "shareholder." These shares are something you own, just as you might own a bicycle or a house.

What is a stock market? A stock market—also called a "stock exchange"—is an organization that gives people the opportunity to buy, sell, or trade shares in an easy, orderly way. An example is the New York Stock Exchange. Countries all over the world have their own stock markets.

How much do stocks cost? All stocks fluctuate in price. The price of a stock is the dollar amount needed to purchase one share of that stock. The price is determined by what investors will pay.

The *bid* price is the highest price offered for a stock at a given time. The *asked* price is the lowest price accepted for that stock at a particular time.

A share can cost a few pennies or more than a hundred dollars. As a rule of thumb, very low-priced stocks are speculative. "Blue chip" stocks are stocks of long-successful, top-rated companies that are known for quality products.

How can owning stocks make you money? Many stocks pay an annual dividend. This is a percentage of the company's profits divided among its stockholders. You can reinvest the amount to purchase more stock, or take the cash. Also, the price of a stock may go up. This often occurs when the company's sales increase. Because the company makes more money, people will pay a higher price for its shares. If you sell the stock for more than you paid, the difference is your profit.

What are bull and bear markets? When the average price of the stock market steadily rises, this is called a "bull market." When it declines, it's a "bear market." Investors who think that the market will go up are called "bulls." Those who think the market is heading down are "bears." An investor can be a bull at one time and a bear at another.

continued ...

How do you purchase a stock?

• *Use a professional stock broker.* A broker is a person who brings together stock buyers and sellers. Each broker works for a brokerage firm. Good stock brokers will discuss your goals and give advice. They will make sure you understand your account statement. You are not charged for those services. Your only cost is a commission when you purchase or sell a stock, about 1% of the transaction.

• *Use a discount broker.* Discount brokers work for discount firms. They may charge a lower commission, but they usually give less service to the investor.

• *Invest online.* This is best left to the experienced investor.

Where can you find information on stocks?

• *Daily newspapers.* In the paper's financial section, you can find information about the economy and about specific companies and their current stock prices. The last price of the day (the closing price) will be listed along with the change from the previous day's price. For example, **GenElec 661/2 + 3/8** means that at the end of the day, General Electric's stock was selling for $66.50 (U.S.) and was 3/8 of a dollar higher than the day before. Some papers print the day's high and low selling prices, since stocks fluctuate during the trading day. If you record this information in a notebook, you can "track" a stock's price over time.

• *Books and magazines.* These are available in most public libraries.

• *Annual reports.* These give information from the companies' managers. You can find a company's address in directories in libraries or on the Internet.

• *The Internet.* There is a great deal of information in cyberspace, but don't believe everything you read on the Web.

• *A stock broker.* If you buy stock through a brokerage company, your broker will supply you with research about the market.

Richard Chadwell has been a stock broker for 42 years and is presently senior vice-president of a major brokerage firm. Following stocks and stock markets is both his job and his hobby.

PART 3

RECREATION

HOW TO Look at a Painting
—by Barbara Guggenheim

Every work of art is a mystery. You can get a painting to reveal its secrets, but this takes work on your part. When I stand in front of a painting, I don't just look at it. I have an imaginary conversation with it. This involves asking and answering lots of questions. As I do this, I move from the unknown to the known, and I realize that I know more than I thought. Here's how you can do the same thing.

DIRECTIONS

1. Begin by asking yourself, "What do I see?" If you were looking at Leonardo da Vinci's famous *Mona Lisa*, you might respond, "Here's a woman wearing a nice dress. She seems rich. She's looking in my direction. She's smiling. She could be 20 or 30."

These details might lead to other questions and thoughts: "Why is she smiling? What could she be thinking about? Maybe someone has said something nice about her. Perhaps she's remembering a dream. Is she wearing black because she's a widow?"

Asking and answering questions requires creativity and concentration. You can't just whiz through a museum. Take your time.

Of course, not every painting has a realistic subject. Suppose you were looking at an abstract painting by Jackson Pollack. You might answer the "What do I see?" question like this: "I see swirls of colors. I see curves. I see blotches of paint." Often it's interesting to step closer to study the texture and other details.

continued ...

2. Next ask, "What does this work of art remind me of?" It may make you think of an experience you've had or a person you know. Or it could remind you of a song or a movie.

Sometimes, one painting will remind me of another painting. If it does, I might compare the two paintings by asking myself, "How are they alike? How are they different?"

3. Now ask yourself, "How do I feel about this painting? Does it make me happy or sad? Does it draw me in or push me away? Do I like it, or dislike it, or just not care?"

4. Look again. It's almost impossible to understand a painting from a single encounter. Try making two circles around the room so that you can "meet" each painting twice.

You can understand why it's not a good idea to try to see everything in a museum in one visit. Pick two or three rooms only. You need time to get to really know a painting. But it's worth it.

Barbara Guggenheim is an art consultant in New York and Los Angeles.

HOW TO Plan a Biking Holiday

—by Henri Slettenhaar

I'm originally from Holland, and biking has always been my favorite sport and means of transport. I now live in France and still like to bicycle. When friends from California were coming to visit me, I decided to plan an eight-day biking tour.

We biked about 30 miles (50 kilometers) a day. Sometimes we stayed for two nights in one place and explored the surroundings. It was the best holiday I ever had. I hope the steps I followed will help you plan a trip for your family or friends.

DIRECTIONS

1. Plan where and when the trip will happen. Start by getting some good maps. Make a daily itinerary with details about the stops and information about the area you'll cross. You can find this information in guidebooks, from tourist offices, and on the Internet. It is nice to know what is happening in the region you will be visiting. We were lucky to find a few fairs and concerts.

2. Test the route ahead of time to find good places to eat and to stay overnight. I did this by car and took my bicycle with me to test some of the routes. I noted the distances and the altitudes. Distance is easy to check from the car's odometer. For the altitude, you need an altimeter. I also checked how busy the roads were. If there was too much traffic, I modified my plans.

continued ...

3. Arrange for a vehicle to accompany the riders. This is important because you do not want to carry your luggage on your bike. It is also practical in case of bad weather, a steep hill, or a problem with a bicycle or rider. On our trip, we had a van that could carry all our luggage, our bikes, and the eight of us (just barely).

4. Make a budget. For a rough estimate, use the data you collected when you tested the route. Add up the hotel, food, and other expenses and divide this amount by the number of participants. Our estimates came to $25 U.S. per day for hotels, $25 a day for food, and $15 a day for other expenses. The total was $65 per day per person.

5. Prepare for emergencies. This includes having spare bicycles, repair gear, a well-stocked first-aid kit to be kept in the vehicle, and a smaller kit to be carried by one of the bikers. It is advisable to have a mobile phone to call for help if necessary. Our van did not follow us like they do in the Tour de France, but was waiting for us about every six miles (10 kilometers). The two people who took care of the van also prepared a delicious picnic lunch for us every day.

6. Plan activities for when you are done biking each day and also in case of rain. Bring small sports equipment and games, for example, a Frisbee, a softball and bat, and cards.

7. Make sure everyone is fit ahead of time. If your friends are out of shape, organize some training before the tour. It is also advisable to have the bicycles checked before you depart. Be sure to include a helmet for each rider.

Have a safe holiday and a lot of fun!

Henri Slettenhaar teaches Computer Science at Webster University in Geneva. He also takes students and computer enthusiasts twice a year to Silicon Valley and got this business idea when he organized the bike tour for his friends. You can reach him by e-mail at slettenhaar@webster.ch.

HOW TO Grow Container Gardens

—by Laura Minnigerode

Even if you live in the city, or don't have an inch of ground to call your own, you can grow vegetables. Lettuce greens, chives, and even edible flowers make a salad fit for a chef! Read on to learn about an easy, three-vegetable garden you can grow in pots wherever you have sun.

DIRECTIONS

1. Nasturtiums, or "nasties" as they are often called, have bright flowers with a peppery smell and taste. The smell is so strong, in fact, that the flowers were originally named because of it. *Nasturtium* comes from the ancient Latin words *nasus*, nose, and *torquere*, to twist. The smell makes your nostrils quiver and twist! Nasturtium petals give salads a peppery taste and lots of color.

In many areas, nasturtiums attract hummingbirds, so keep your eyes peeled!

• *Nasturtium Growing Tip*: Make sure your seedlings get 4 to 6 hours of sun.

2. Lettuce comes in many varieties that grow well in containers. These include Simpson, Oakleaf, Salad Bowl, and Ruby. Ask at your garden store for the varieties that grow well in your area.

• *Lettuce Growing Tip*: The best pot for lettuce growing is at least 20 inches (50 cm) around and 12 inches (30 cm) deep. Get creative. You can use a Styrofoam cooler, a half wine barrel, or a cardboard box lined with a plastic bag. Punch holes in the bottom and in the plastic liner to provide drainage.

continued ...

SALAD WITH FLOWERS

Make a salad that looks like a flower garden!
You'll need
• nasturtium petals
• lettuce leaves
• snipped chives
• 1/4 cup (.06 l) toasted sunflower seeds

Combine the petals, lettuce, and chives in a salad bowl. Top with the seeds. Serve with your favorite dressing.

3. Chives (the word is singular) is a type of onion. All onions, by the way, are members of the lily family. Plant the seeds in a four-inch (10 cm) container, and sprinkle some soil mix over them. Use a plant mister to wet the soil. Cover the container with waxed paper or plastic wrap.

After the seedlings have sprouted, you may need to thin them, leaving only one per container. Snip the tops finely, and use them on a baked potato or in your incredible edible salad.

• *Chives Growing Tip*: You can grow chives indoors too! Since it is a perennial (lasts more than one year), keep it indoors on a windowsill all winter.

CHIVE VINEGAR
• 2 cups (.5 l) white vinegar
• 1 tablespoon (15 ml) chive blossoms
(pulled from stems)
Combine the blossoms with vinegar. Strain petals when using. The petals will turn the vinegar a pretty pink color and give an onion flavor.

SOIL MATES
All dirt is not created equal! Since the soil provides plants with a home and food, gardeners try to match the soil to each plant's needs. For your lettuce and vegetables, you'll want to provide soil that doesn't hold extra water, but instead lets it drain. Here's a recipe to make a bushel (35 l) of potting mixture. The ingredients are available at garden stores.

Horticultural vermiculite	1/2 bushel (17.5 l)
Peat moss	1/2 bushel (17.5 l)
Ground limestone	5 tablespoons (75 ml)
Organic fertilizer	10 tablespoons (150 ml)
Powdered superphosphate	2 teaspoons (10 ml)

Laura Minnigerode is Youth Garden Coordinator for Urban Harvest, a community gardening network in Houston, Texas. She's also the author of *The Kid-Friendly Web Guide*, and is founder of a kids' online garden club. For information, write LMinniger@aol.com.

HOW TO Pack for a  Trip

—by Betty Winsett

Successful traveling depends a lot on what you take and how you pack it. Luckily, smart packing is easy.

DIRECTIONS

1. A week before you leave, make a packing list. Starting early gives you time to remember things. Once you have your list, study it. Cross out as many items as possible. The lighter you travel, the happier you'll be.

2. Choose your luggage carefully. No one enjoys carrying a large, unwieldy piece. I prefer the type with wheels that flight crews often use.

3. Pack at least a day before departing. Place your opened luggage on a flat surface, along with all the items you plan to take. Keep your packing list handy. As you place each item in the bag, check it off your list.

• Pack heavy things on the side with the wheels. These include electronic items and shoes (stored in a plastic bag so they don't soil your clothing).

• Lay out pants, skirts, dresses, shirts, and blouses. To prevent creases, place socks or underwear at the place where each garment is to be folded. Fold the clothes but do not pack yet!

• Pack soft items, like robes, above the heavy items.

• Place the folded clothing above the soft items. Belts can go around the walls of the bag.

• If your luggage has inside straps, fasten these over the clothing to keep the garments from shifting.

• Place your name and address on both the inside and the outside of your bag.

4. Carry your bag around your home. If it's too heavy, look for items to remove.

PACKING LIST
• Outer clothing
• Night clothes
• Raincoat
• Hat
• Shoes & socks
• Underwear
• Belt
• Jewelry
• Camera & film
• Toiletries
• Sunscreen
• Insect repellant
• Games
• Books
• Hair dryer
• Gifts
• Laundry bag
• Maps
• Travel guides
• Phone numbers

TRAVEL TIPS

• *Clothing:* Smart travelers take as few clothes as possible. Choose color-coordinated garments that you can mix and match. If weather permits, a sweater can replace a heavy jacket. For a raincoat, take one of those plastic types that fold into a tiny space. Wear or carry bulky clothes to save space in your bag. Consider wearing older clothes that you can discard or give away on the trip to make room for new clothes and souvenirs.

• *Laundry:* If you wash clothing by hand, after rinsing and wringing as well as you can, roll it in a towel. This will remove much excess moisture and allow the item to dry faster. Many experienced travelers—including males—take silk underwear because it dries quickly.

• *Liquids:* Put liquids like shampoo in plastic containers, which are lighter than glass and won't break. For extra safety, put the containers into zippered freezer bags.

• *Photography:* When taking photographs through glass and using a flash, stand at an angle. Otherwise you will get a picture of your flash, not exactly what you are hoping for.

• *Film:* Because film is often expensive when bought at tourist sites, bring more than you think you'll need.

• *Souvenir/gift space:* Pack an empty flight bag folded flat. You can fill it later with items you buy.

• *Gifts:* If you will be staying at someone's home, it's always courteous to bring a gift.

• *Electronics:* If you're going to a foreign country, be sure your hair dryer or other electronic equipment has the right voltage, or get a converter and an adaptor.

• *Towels:* You may want to bring an extra towel for your hair or to use for drying your underwear after washing it.

• *Journal:* To help recall your trip years later, keep a daily record of what you do, see, and think. Some of the world's most famous travelers have done this, including Marco Polo and Christopher Columbus.

Betty Winsett has traveled to all seven continents, including Antarctica. When not traveling, she teaches computer and Internet skills.

HOW TO Ride a Horse
—by Carol Moore

"Horseback riding is easy enough," cowboys say. "Put a leg on each side, keep your mind in the middle, take a deep seat and a faraway look, and away we go." If you need a little more instruction, I'll give you enough information to accomplish a gentle trail ride in the western style.

DIRECTIONS

1. Know the jargon. A horse's headgear is a bridle, the piece in his mouth is a bit, and the reins are what you hold for control. The saddle is what you will be sitting on.

2. To mount, approach your horse from his left. With someone holding the horse and supporting the saddle, face the horse with your right shoulder next to its left side. Place your left foot in the stirrup, put your left hand on the saddle horn and right hand on the back of the saddle, and hop. Settle into the deepest part of the seat.

3. Pick up the reins in one hand. Hold them as you would an ice cream cone: little finger towards the horse's neck, thumb on top, knuckles facing towards the ears. Your hand should be just above and in front of the saddle horn. In fact, at a walk you may rest your wrist on the horn.

continued ...

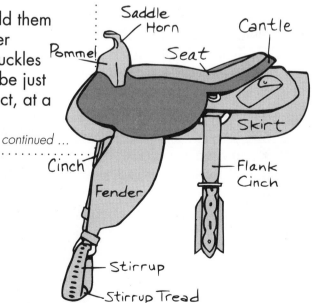

Saddle Horn
Cantle
Pommel
Seat
Skirt
Cinch
Flank Cinch
Fender
Stirrup
Stirrup Tread

4. Wait for your assistant to adjust your stirrups. The bottom of the stirrup should be about even with your instep. Place the ball of your foot on each stirrup, and let your feet hang directly under you. You should be able to see the tip of your toe when looking over your knee. For good position and balance, keep your heel slightly lower than your toe. Always keep even weight on both stirrups.

5. To move forward, apply heel pressure. Turn your toes out, bring your heels near the horse's body, and bump him gently just behind the saddle cinch as if elbowing someone. Increase the pressure to achieve the desired response. Forward movement must be accompanied by your reaching forward to slacken the reins.

6. Use neck reining to steer. To make a right-hand turn, reach your hand forward and pull the reins across to the right. To make a left, reach forward and to the left. If you forget, point your thumb in the direction you wish to go and follow it with your hand and the reins.

7. To motivate the horse to turn, use heel pressure. Horses generally move away from pressure, so use your right heel for a left turn and left heel for a right turn.

8. To stop, pull the reins back toward your belt buckle. If you are not able to achieve a stop by the time your hand is past the saddle horn, your reins are probably too long. Make an adjustment by taking your free hand and pulling the reins through your hand to the desired length. The reins control the horse by pulling on his mouth and tightening the curb strap at the same time.

9. To back up, apply a steady backward pull on the reins. Release this pressure to make the horse stop backing up.

10. Pay attention while riding. Treat horses with respect. They are about 10 times your size and can be dangerous. Don't get involved in roughhousing or careless horseplay. Make your ride a safe and fun experience for all.

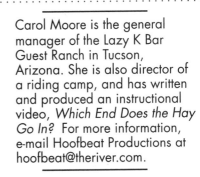

Carol Moore is the general manager of the Lazy K Bar Guest Ranch in Tucson, Arizona. She is also director of a riding camp, and has written and produced an instructional video, *Which End Does the Hay Go In?* For more information, e-mail Hoofbeat Productions at hoofbeat@theriver.com.

HOW TO Be a Roller Coaster Critic

—by Sam Marks

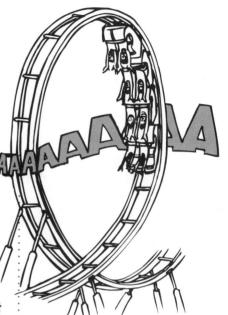

Critics try to help people understand and enjoy things, such as movies, plays, and concerts. I'm a critic of roller coasters. If you love these wonderful constructions as much as I do, you too can become a coaster critic. Hold on tight, and I'll teach you how.

DIRECTIONS

1. Know your coaster history.

• During winters, 19th-century Russians poured water on sloping structures and created ice slides.

• Later, the French locked cars to downhill tracks.

• Near the start of the 20th century, LeMarcus Thompson, called the "father of the gravity ride," built the Switchback Railway at Coney Island, New York. It had a top speed of six miles (10 kilometers) per hour. Although sometimes dangerous, these thrill rides became the rage.

2. Understand the main coaster types.

• *Wooden coasters*, dating back 100 years, have a wood structure and track. Steel rails keep the wheels from cutting grooves in the wood.

• *Steel coasters*, developed in the 1970s, feature a metal structure, tubular steel tracks, and fiberglass cars on steel chassis. Thanks to strong materials, steel coasters often include loops and corkscrews that turn riders upside down. Steel hypercoasters, first built in the 1980s, feature hills more than 200 feet (60 meters) high.

• *Stand-up coasters*, dating from the 1980s, use high-tech safety restraints. One turns riders upside down five times!

3. To judge a coaster fairly, ride it at least twice. Try both the front car and the last car.

continued ...

RIDE SAFELY

Coasters are safe if you follow a few simple rules:

• Always stay seated.

• Keep arms and legs inside the vehicle.

• Make sure all the safety devices, such as the seat belt, are properly functioning.

4. Grade the coaster's features. Here's a list that can be scored from 0 (bad) to 10 (great).

• *Acceleration*: How fast do you feel you're going? Because of twists and turns, one coaster can *feel* faster than another even though it isn't as fast.

• *Duration*: How long does it last? A long ride is not always great, but if two coasters are equal in other ways, the one that lasts longer gets a plus.

• *Gravity effects*: Is your stomach in your throat or in your lap? A coaster can make you feel weightless (technically called "negative g"), or it can push you into the seat (called "positive g"). You can even experience a side-to-side push ("lateral g"). All these feelings can provide thrills.

• *Sound*: Do you hear a clinking noise going up the lift hill? Creaking, clackety sounds can add fun. Some coasters throw in recorded sound effects.

• *View*: Are you above the trees? Some coasters give you a beautiful view at the top of the first hill.

• *Scare factor*: Do you have white knuckles from holding on? Is it the height, curves, loops, or a combination of things that makes you feel like you are in danger?

• *Special features*: What extras are there? Modern designers use multimedia effects, such as flashing lights, fog, and the dark (for coasters in buildings). There's also external "theming," for example, creating a coaster in the shape of a mountain.

5. Write your review. Don't just give your overall opinion. Describe the features you liked or didn't like. Send your review to friends, or try to get it published in a newspaper or on the Web.

Sam Marks has ridden hundreds of coasters. He founded the Coaster Zombies Club. His Web site is http://members.aol.com/Steelforce/index.html.

SAM'S FAVORITES

• Wooden coaster: "The Riverside Cyclone" at Riverside Park, Agawam, MA: the meanest piece of wood rolling today!

• Steel coaster: "Steel Force" at Dorney Park, Allentown, PA: smooth, fast, scary with lots of neg, pos, and lateral g's.

• Scariest coaster: "Alpengeist" at Busch Gardens, Williamsburg, VA: nicknamed "Fear-n-Height."

• Best view: "Magnum XL 200" at Cedar Point, Sandusky, OH: you can see across Lake Erie to Canada!

• Most unusual: "Viper" at Six Flags Great Adventure, Jackson, NJ: steel rings encircle the track, giving a high-speed sensation.

• Fastest: "Steel Phantom" at Kennywood, West Mifflin, PA: the second drop goes under a hill of the Thunderbolt wood roller coaster.

• Ultimate all-out greatest coaster in the world: "Steel Force."

HOW TO Train a Dog to Catch a *Frisbee*

—by Keith and Lori Friend

No one is born knowing how to catch a Frisbee. But almost anyone can learn how to do it, including dogs. Teaching your dog to catch a sailing disc will come in handy when you don't have a human to play with. It'll also give your pet plenty of wholesome exercise. As you work through the following steps, remember that the training should be done only when your dog is eager. If the dog loses interest or gets tired, put the Frisbee aside for a while. Then try again later.

DIRECTIONS

1. Train your dog in basic obedience.

Important commands are "Stay," "Come," "Look," and "Retrieve" or "Get it." The last command is handy when you don't feel like picking up the 42 Frisbees you just scattered all over the yard. We highly recommend an obedience class. This will help you on and off the Frisbee field.

2. Get your dog acquainted with the Frisbee.

Try to get your dog excited about taking the Frisbee in his mouth. One strategy is to feed your dog out of a Frisbee to get him used to having the Frisbee near his mouth. Whenever the dog's teeth touch the Frisbee, say, "Take" or a similar command that will regularly be used to get the dog to grab the Frisbee. The "Take" command teaches the dog to grab the disc on command.

continued ...

3. Roll the Frisbee along the ground in front of your dog. This gives your dog practice in chasing and grabbing the moving disc. If your dog is like ours, he might chase the Frisbee but not want to bring it back. In this case, use a "long line," a leash of at least 15 feet (5 meters). When your dog grabs the Frisbee, just reel him in. Give a command such as "Bring it" and act excited. Do this about a million times, and your dog will behave like a Labrador retriever.

4. Teach your dog to release the Frisbee after retrieving it. Hold the Frisbee with one hand. With your other hand, grasp your dog's jaw just behind the Frisbee and squeeze. Important: Use a command such as "Drop" or "Out" every time you do this. When he lets go, praise him like he's just done the best dog trick of all time. Soon, he'll be dropping the disc on command. Hint: Stop playing "tug of war" with your dog. Sure, it's fun, but he doesn't know the difference between a sock and a Frisbee.

5. Practice accurate throwing. In canine Frisbee, you are half the team. It's as important for you to throw the Frisbee accurately as it is for your dog to catch it consistently. Go with a human friend and learn how to throw the Frisbee on target. Try different types of throws (forehand, backhand, over the head, behind the back, etc.). Using different throws scores higher in competitions.

6. Play catch. Hold the Frisbee at arm's length above your dog's head and say, "Take." If he won't rise up to grab it, lower it a little. Say your "Take" command each time he touches the Frisbee. As your dog gets good at grabbing the Frisbee out of your hand, raise it a little, and drop the disc just before he grabs it. Then, toss the disc in front of your dog. Start with short throws. Then work up to throwing it as far as you can. Gradually work in fancy tosses, such as behind the back and under the leg throws. With practice, your dog will be catching the Frisbee like a champ.

Canine Frisbee is a great sport and builds a tight bond between you and your dog. But if it's hot, give your dog lots of water, and let him cool down before he gets overheated. Your dog may not know when to stop playing, so you must make that decision for him.

Keith and Lori Friend are members of The Dallas Dog and Disc Club. They perform at football games and other exhibitions. For more about Frisbee dogs, including animations, visit The Dallas Dog and Disc Club Web site at:http://rampages.onramp.net/~friend/dddpage.html.

HOW TO Sand SCULPT

—by Mark Mason

Have you ever packed a bucket with wet sand, turned it over, and made a castle? I've taken these simple techniques, added a few tricks, and won many sand sculpting prizes including first place at the World Sand Sculpting Championship held in British Columbia, Canada. Follow my secrets and you too can make intricate sand sculptures that gather crowds and win contests.

DIRECTIONS

1. Have an adult use the utility knife to cut the bottom from one bucket. Cut from the bottom, not the side, to leave a rim of sturdy plastic.

2. Take the materials to a beach, a sand box, or other sandy spot. To sculpt at home, get clean but "un-washed" sand from a sand and gravel pit.

3. Place the bottomless bucket upside down.

4. Shovel in 3 inches (8 cm) of sand.

5. Fill the second bucket with water and pour enough into the first to get the layer of sand real wet.

6. Mix the wet sand with your fingers. It's important to make sure all the sand gets evenly wet.

7. Use the board to tamp down the sand hard. The bucket keeps it from spreading and increases the surface tension, forcing the grains of sand tightly together. That's the secret to making your sculpture last longer, even after it dries out.

8. Add more sand layers 3 inches (8 cm) at a time. Thoroughly wet and mix the sand before tamping it down. Continue until the bucket is full.

continued ...

MATERIALS
- shovel
- two 5-gallon (20 l) plastic buckets
- 2"x 4" (5 cm x 10 cm) piece of wood about 2' (.5 m) long
- small paintbrush
- utility knife
- spatula
- melon baller
- cake icing spreader
- drinking straw

9. Tap lightly around the outside, including the bottom ridges. Slip the bucket up and off by pulling from the bottom ridges. You'll now have a tightly packed, bucket-shaped pile of sand, layered like the strata on the side of a cliff. If you see air pockets, you didn't tamp the sand hard enough or you made the layers too thick. Repack the sand.

10. Decide what to carve. You can make anything from sand, such as a pet or an image seen in a magazine. As an example, let's sculpt a rabbit.

11. Grab a handful of wet sand. Shape an ear just off center on top of your sand pile.

12. Place a smaller handful next to it. Shape a second ear, this one flopped over. With the ears set you should be able to picture the bunny's face.

13. Carve the nose. Be ready to cut away lots of the packed sand. You're releasing the bunny from inside the bucket shape. Experiment with the tools:
• Use the spatula to shape surfaces.
• Use the melon baller for scooping even-sized holes and half circles for textures. Also, use it to add buttons, noses, rivets, and such from sand packed in the tool and knocked out.
• Use the cake icing spreader for details.
• Use the brush to smooth areas and erase marks.
• Use the straw to blow off small debris and to make small eyes and half circles as textures.

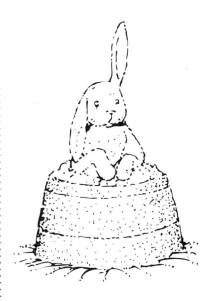

BONUS TIPS
• Undercut your sculpture for interesting shadows.
• Carve a scene at the sculpture's base. For example, try a moat and roads around a castle.
• Use a large plastic garbage can to make a giant sculpture. Cut the bottom as you did the bucket and pack the can layer by layer.
• Take photos for a scrapbook. Later you can view your first sculptures and see how far you've come.

Mark Mason's company Sand-tastic Promotions holds a Guinness World Record in sand sculpture. Based in Sarasota, Florida, Mark and his team travel the globe creating unique promotions and leading "Professional Sand Sculpture Clinics." Visit their Web site at http://members.aol.com/sandsculpt.

HOW TO Throw a Boomerang

—by Alison Fujino

I grew up in a baseball family and learned to throw baseballs, and everything else. Years later, while working at the Smithsonian Institution in Washington, D.C., I found a collection of boomerangs. (Experts call them "sticks.") By luck, my boss, Benjamin Ruhe, was a great boomerang master. Thanks to Ben's teaching, I became the first woman to win an international boomerang title.

Throwing a boomerang is only a bit more complicated than tossing a Frisbee, but worth the effort. There is something magical about sending the stick on its way and watching it return.

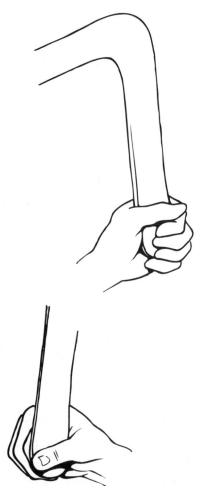

BE SAFE

Choose a large and flat field, free of obstructions, such as trees. You need at least 100 yards (100 meters) of clear space in all directions. Before throwing, make sure that no one has entered your throwing area!

DIRECTIONS

1. Get a well-made boomerang. Also, you'll need one that matches your throwing hand, because there are left-handed and right-handed boomerangs.

2. Choose a calm day. For best results, do not practice when there is more than a gentle breeze.

3. Pick up the stick with the flat side facing your palm. Hold it by the wing tip, using a full or a pinch grip:
• *Full grip*: Rest the boomerang on your little finger with your other fingers curled around it.
• *Pinch grip*: Pinch the end with your thumb and fingers.

4. Hold the boomerang vertically (up and down) or nearly so. Never hold it in a horizontal or flat position as you would hold a Frisbee.

continued ...

5. Aim 100 yards (100 meters) out. Position your boomerang and arm just above eye level.

6. Cock the boomerang over your shoulder with your elbow bent. Step forward on the opposite foot and launch outward. Extend your upper arm as if cracking a whip. Keep your arm close to your head to prevent *sidearming* the boomerang. For success, the launch must be almost vertical.

7. Snap your wrist at the last moment when your arm is extended. Don't open your hand to release the boomerang. When your wrist snaps, this creates the all-important spin as the stick *pulls* out of your hand. Spinning like a gyroscope, the boomerang will climb a bit, lie flat, and circle back to you. Spin counts more than power. If you have difficulty adding spin to your throw, grip the boomerang as tightly as you can. Don't worry about it sticking to your hand: it will pull itself free with loads of extra snap. After practicing, you will find that the steps become a natural progression.

8. Use your hands like a sandwich to trap the returning boomerang. To keep your chest and fingers from getting hit, pull it away from your body. If the boomerang is coming in too fast, move to the side. Do not put up your hand to block it.

Alison Fujino has competed in boomerang competitions throughout the world. She is the mother of two boys (who throw everything), and is an active boomerang collector and chucker.

BOOMERANG COMPETITIONS

Boomerang contests include a variety of events:
- *Consecutive Catch*: Throw and catch a boomerang five times. The winner does it in the shortest time. The record is about 11 seconds!
- *Juggling*: Throw a boomerang, and before it returns, throw another. Keep going until missing. The record is about 600 catches.
- *Maximum Time Aloft*: Use a special boomerang that climbs and can stay up for about five minutes. You must catch it, so you need great foot work.
- *Distance*: The goal is to see who can throw the farthest and back for a catch.

HOW TO Watch a Ball Game

—by Leonard Koppett

Everybody knows that you're supposed to "keep your eye on the ball." The television camera follows that rule almost all the time. No wonder. Ultimately, the score depends on where the ball ends up—over the goal line, through the basket, or over the fence. But much more is going on, especially in major league games. You can increase your enjoyment and understanding as a spectator by paying attention to a few additional items. Here's what to look for.

DIRECTIONS

Baseball. Before a pitch, note how the fielders have positioned themselves: more towards right, more towards left, or "straightaway"; closer to or further from home; all the same way or in different combinations. This tells you where they *expect* the ball to be hit, and how the pitcher hopes to make the batter hit the ball that way.

Basketball. Watch what happens *immediately after* the ball goes through the basket instead of automatically shifting your attention to the other end of the floor. That's where the next play takes shape. That first pass after the scored-upon team takes possession will tell you about the offense—whether it will be a fast break or a play to be developed past mid-court—and the defense—whether it is pressing or simply dropping back.

continued ...

American Football. Don't worry about how the defense lines up for a play: it's trying to fool the offense until the last moment. But watch the offensive formation for a clue to the play: bunched up or spread out, more to one side or another, or in some unusual pattern. Also, focus on the area three or four yards directly *behind* the center: every play must start there, with a handoff or setting up to pass, regardless of "formations." If the passer is rushed hard, a passing game can't succeed. If his blockers give him time, it can. Finally, when a play is over, note where the front-line pile is as the players get up. If it's a few yards beyond where the play started, the offense is winning the physical battle. If it's still where the line of scrimmage was, the defense is winning.

Every sport has features of this type. Learn what they are, and you'll start to see *why* things happen as well as what happens. Even in individual sports—the first serve in tennis, putting in golf—certain actions play a key role in winning. By learning how to notice them, you can become a more satisfied and better-informed spectator.

Leonard Koppett spent many years as a sports columnist for *The New York Times.* He is the author of several books on sports.

HOW TO Fly a KITE

—by Corey Jensen

Diamond

Delta

Parafoil

Box

Dragon

Kite flyers know that a kite has no "spirit" until it has been flown. Even if your kite is for decoration, it should be flown at least once. Kite flying is great fun and it's easy if you know a few secrets. So grab your kite and join in the fun. The sky is big enough for everyone!

DIRECTIONS

1. Pick a kite and assemble it correctly. There are many different kinds. Kite flyers carry different types of kites for different winds. Enjoy the different experiences each type offers.

• Deltas, Diamonds, and Dragon kites fly well in light to medium winds (6 - 12 miles per hour/10 - 20 kilometers per hour).

• Box kites need more wind or a pair of wings for added lift.

• Parafoils are soft kites, inflated by the wind. They fly better when the winds are medium (8 - 15 miles per hour/13 - 24 kilometers per hour). Larger kites often fly in lighter winds.

2. Pick good kite days. Learn to watch for the right kite-flying conditions. Wind that is too strong or too light is difficult to fly in. About 6 - 15 miles per hour (10 - 24 kilometers per hour) is best for most kites (when leaves and bushes start to move, but before it really starts to blow). Kite flying is most fun when the wind is medium so you can do more than just hold on. You can make your kite dance across the sky by pulling in and letting out the line.

continued ...

FLY SAFE!
• Don't fly near power lines, airports, or roads.
• Avoid storms. Never fly in rain or lightning. Electricity in clouds is attracted to damp kite lines and foolish kite flyers.
DON'T EXPERIMENT!

3. Know where to fly. Always fly in a clear, open area. Stay away from roads, power lines, and airports. Open fields, parks, and beaches are great for flying kites. The more room you have, the more line you can let out. Remember that as wind goes around trees and buildings, it gets bumpy and difficult to fly kites in. Watch out for kite-eating trees, too!

4. Know how to fly a single-line kite.
Stand with your back to the wind. Hold your kite up by the bridle point and let the line out. If there is sufficient wind, your kite will go right up. Let the kite fly away from you a little, then pull in on the line as the kite points up so it will climb. Repeat this until your kite gains the altitude necessary to find a good steady wind.

• If there's a light wind, have a helper take the kite downwind (away from you in the direction the wind is blowing) and hold it up. On command, the helper releases the kite and the flyer pulls the line hand-over-hand while the kite gains altitude. Practice this "high launch" technique.

• If you don't have a helper, prop the kite up against a bush, post, or wall. Reel out enough line for altitude and simply pull the kite aloft.

• If the kite sinks tail first, there might not be enough wind. If it comes down head first or spins, there might be too much wind. Different kites fly in different winds.

• If your kite has an adjustable bridle, move it higher (nearer the top) in higher winds, and lower (towards the tail) in lower winds. Adjust no more than .5 inch (1.3 cm) at a time.

• If the kite seems unstable, especially in stronger winds, adding tails can help. Use lightweight materials so you can use lots! Colorful tails streaming across the sky look great!

continued ...

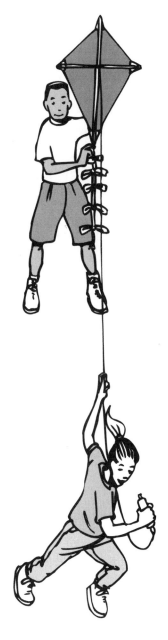

5. Know how to fly an acrobatic kite.

• *Lay out your stunter and lines completely before you launch, with the kite downwind.* Be sure you have enough room. Check all connectors, unsnarl and straighten lines and tails.

• *Check the bridles.* Be sure they are adjusted correctly for the present conditions.

• *Be sure you have enough line.* Use at least 60 - 100 feet (18 - 30 m) so you have time to react. Be sure your flying lines are even. If one line is shorter, your kite will think you are pulling that line and spin in that direction.

• *To launch, step backwards and pull both handles to your side.* Be sure to check behind you for obstructions or hazards before backing up.

• *To control the flight direction, pull on the lines.* Pull the left line to make the stunter turn left. Pull the right to turn it right. Hold the lines even to fly the kite straight. Try not to over-control. Learn to "fly loops" instead of just spinning tight circles.

• *Orient yourself to the wind.* The more to the side of the wind the stunter flies, the less lift and speed it has. While learning to fly, keep the stunter downwind. As you get better, explore more subtle levels of performance.

• *Fly safely.* Always stay away from spectators and passersby. You are responsible for the safe operation of your stunter. Sport kites should never be flown in crowded areas.

PROFESSOR KITE'S HELPFUL HINTS

• Fly away from other people.

• If you tangle lines with another kite, don't yank the line or it might break. Flyers should walk together and the tangle will slide right down the line to where you can unwrap it.

• As your skills grow, offer to help a friend. Flying is fun. Pass it on.

• Always think about safety. Never endanger yourself or others.

• Slow down, take it easy, and enjoy!

Corey Jensen lives in windy Pacific Grove, California. In 1988, he served as president of the American Kitefliers Association (www.aka.kite.org) and has served as announcer at kite events around the world. He is also the creator of Professor Kite. His e-mail address is coreykite@aol.com.

Many wonderful people just like you enjoy the pleasures and fellowship to be found at the end of a kite line. Sharing seems to make the fun even greater. See you in the sky!

HOW TO Improve Your Soccer Game
—by David Hale

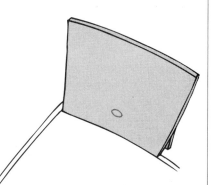

Over the years, I've coached many players in soccer (or "football" as it's known around the world). But talented or not, most players don't excel at the game for two reasons: One, they can't stop the ball and control it right at their feet, and two, they're unable to pass accurately on the ground, even over a short distance.

Racing down the field and shooting may seem exciting. But efficient scoring depends on ball control and passing. These skills are the keys to teamwork. If you can stop the ball and send it to a fellow player, you'll experience the true joy of the game. Luckily, you can easily sharpen your skills through solo practice. All it takes is a ball, a wall, and a half hour a day.

DIRECTIONS

1. Use chalk to draw a target on the wall.

2. Practice passing the ball toward your spot. Use the inside of the foot, not the toe.

3. Practice ball control. When the ball bounces back, run after it and stop it at your feet. Keep it from bouncing away. Then aim and pass at your spot again.

4. Continue the activity. Because the ball comes off the wall at many angles, and because you'll reach it at various distances from the wall, you'll practice passing from the right and the left, from close and far.

This simple activity has great value. You'll be busy every second. You won't have to wait for someone to send you the ball. You won't be distracted by small talk. You'll concentrate entirely on doing what every great soccer player must do: stop and control the ball, and send it accurately on its way.

David Hale played soccer in college and on a semi-pro team in San Jose, California. A graphic designer by trade, he has also raced sports cars.

HOW TO Build a Model Boat
—by Dudley Lewis

A boat, large or small, is nothing more than a box that keeps water out. It floats because its shape displaces (pushes aside) an amount of water that weighs more than the boat. The displaced water pushes back and lifts the boat.

To study flotation, roll clay into a small ball and try to float it in a glass of water. Now, form the clay into the shape of a boat and try to float it.

When I was six, a carpenter taught me how to build a model boat. I didn't know anything when I started, but knew a lot when I finished. Now, I'd like to share that knowledge with you.

Materials
- 3 sheets of paper of the same size, for example, photocopy or computer paper
- wood glue
- small nails
- hammer
- safety glasses
- caulk (latex)
- 1/4 inch (6 mm) plywood
- paint and paintbrush
- sponge or cloth

DIRECTIONS

1. Use the three pieces of paper to create the patterns you'll need to cut the wood.
- Fold one sheet in half lengthwise, along its long axis. Cut this piece of paper in half, along the fold. These two halves are patterns for the long sides of your model boat.
- Fold a second sheet into thirds, along its shorter axis. Cut this piece of paper into thirds, along the folds. Two of these pieces are patterns for the front (bow) and back (stern) of your model. Don't worry if the bow and stern pieces are different widths than the sides.
- Keep the third, whole sheet of paper as a pattern for the bottom of your model.

2. Bring your paper patterns to a lumber yard. Have pieces of 1/4 inch (6 mm) plywood cut to match the patterns.

continued ...

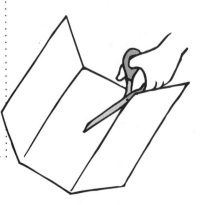

3. Back in your work area, construct the model.

Use only water-based carpentry glue and latex paint. Petroleum-based glues and paints are not recommended.

- Stand the two side pieces of wood on end as shown.
- Apply a thin line of glue along the edge of one piece.
- Place the bottom piece on top of the two sides. Be sure the outside edge of the sides lines up with the outside edge of the bottom. The side that is not yet glued acts as a support when you start nailing.
- Put on the safety glasses because when you start nailing, splinters or nails may fly into your face.
- Gently nail through the bottom piece, connecting it to the edge that has the glue. Start at one end and work toward the other end, placing a nail every two inches (5 cm). Wipe off any excess glue.

If you don't know how to use a hammer, ask someone who does for instruction. Then practice hammering nails into scrap wood. Keep your fingers out of the way.

- Apply glue along the edge of the other side and nail it to the bottom as you did with the first piece.
- Stand the pieces you just put together on end. Glue and nail the bow to your model.
- Flip the model onto its other end. Glue and nail the stern to the model. Let the glue dry.

4. Make your model watertight.

- Apply a thin bead of caulk along the inside edges of your boat. Be sure the caulk covers the seams between the bottom and the sides, the bow, and the stern. Wipe off the leftover caulk with a damp sponge. Allow the caulk to dry.

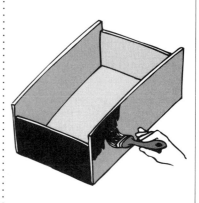

- Paint the boat inside and out. This will keep the wood from swelling, and it will give the boat an appealing look. For best results, begin with two coats of primer, a special paint designed for bare wood. It creates a coat that regular paint can stick to. After the primer coats dry, add two coats of enamel paint.

You're now ready to take your model on its maiden voyage. After you test it, you might later try building larger boats and adding details, such as sails, keel, and rudder.

Dudley Lewis is a carpenter and handyman. He has built several full-size boats and many houses. When not building things for other people, he spends time remodeling his home, a Victorian cottage in Santa Cruz, California.

HOW TO Make a Telescope

—by Stephen J. Edberg

In 1609, Galileo built the first telescope used to study the heavens. With only a little effort, you can make a telescope similar to Galileo's. Depending on the materials, it will have magnification from about 11x to 33x. An 11x telescope gives an image that is 11 times bigger than what you'd see using the naked eye. You'll be working with the same scientific principles used by astronomers to build instruments like the huge 200-inch (5-meter) telescope at Palomar Mountain and the Hubble Space Telescope.

MATERIALS
- lens
- 8x photographer's loupe
- mailing tube or plastic pipe
- knife or saw
- ruler or tape measure
- masking tape

DIRECTIONS

1. Select a mailing tube. The outer diameter should be at least 2 inches (5 cm) and no more than about 2.5 inches (6 cm). The tube's length will depend on the magnification you want. For greater magnification, you need a longer tube. As a first effort, choose one of the following tube lengths:
- 42 inches (105 cm) for a 33x telescope
- 22 inches (55 cm) for a 17x telescope
- 15 inches (38 cm) for an 11x telescope

2. Buy the lens. At an eyeglass store, order a full-size lens with the same diameter as—or slightly larger than—the outer diameter of the tube. The lens should match the power of the telescope you're building. You need:
- a 1 diopter lens to build a 33x telescope
- a 2 diopter lens to build a 17x telescope
- a 3 diopter lens to build an 11x telescope

If you buy the lens at a camera store, you'll use different terms. Ask for a close-up lens of +1, +2, or +3. You may have to buy a whole set.

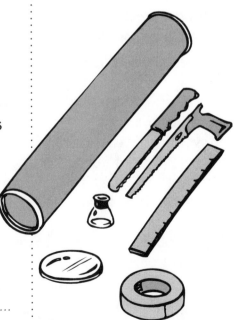

continued ...

3. At the camera store, purchase an 8x loupe with a flat base. A loupe is used by photographers to examine negatives or prints. For our purposes, the loupe becomes the eyepiece of the telescope.

4. Back in your work space, carefully use a knife or saw to trim the tube down to the starting size. Further trimming may be needed for final adjustments. Caution: If you haven't had lots of experience using a knife or saw, find an expert to make the cuts.

5. Use masking tape to attach the lens to one end of the tube. The "bulge" (convex side) of the lens should face away from the tube. Cover only the outer edge of the lens with tape: you don't want the lens to fall off but you also want to obscure as little of the glass as possible, just the portion already blocked by the tube.

6. Wrap tape around the base of the loupe so that it slides smoothly but snugly into the tube.

7. Test the telescope. Look at something across the street. What you see will not only look closer but also be upside down. That's the way single-lens telescopes work. It's not a problem when studying heavenly bodies, because there's no "up" or "down" in space.

To get sharp focus, push the loupe in. If that doesn't help, you'll have to take the scope apart and shorten the tube slightly. Now look at something in the distance. The loupe will probably need to be moved in again.

8. Keep the scope steady. Try leaning it against something, or mount it to a camera tripod.

Stephen J. Edberg is an astronomer at NASA's Jet Propulsion Laboratory. He is also Executive Director of the Riverside Telescope Makers Conference.

Now you're ready to look at the moon, the planets, and the stars. There are amazing new worlds for you to discover with your telescope. Explore and enjoy!

HOW TO Sharpen Your Chess Skills

—by Peter J. Kurzdorfer

King

Queen

Bishop

Rook

Knight

Pawn

Long ago, chess was a favorite among royalty. It's still sometimes called the "royal game." However, these days all sorts of people play chess, from pre-schoolers to senior citizens. I know of no other sport where 10-year-olds can compete on even terms with 40-year-olds, or even with a three-year-old computer program! And players can compete with opponents around the world by way of the Internet.

Besides fun, chess gives practice in critical thinking and problem solving. As with dance, painting, and other creative activities, you can learn chess basics quickly, then spend a lifetime improving your skills.

There are many ways to become good at chess: find someone to coach you; read books, such as *Bobby Fischer Teaches Chess*; and join a chess club.

One of the best methods is to study the thinking of great players by replaying their games. Here's how to do it.

DIRECTIONS

1. Learn how to identify each square on the board. See page 89.

2. Make sure you know the name and the initial of each piece and how the piece moves. Again, see page 89.

3. Choose a game to replay. For now, use the game presented on pages 90 and 91. You can find many other games in chess books.

4. As you replay a game, think about each move before reading the notes. Ask yourself why the player made the move. Then choose a next move and compare it with the actual move.

CHESS BASICS

Chessboard

A chessboard consists of 64 squares. In the numbering system that I use, each file (vertical set of squares) is labeled by a letter. Each rank (horizontal set of squares) is numbered. Each square is named by a letter-number combination such as **d5**. (See examples on next page.)

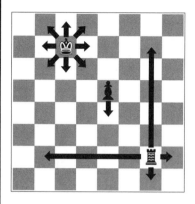

King (K): The king moves one square at a time on any diagonal, rank, or file. If it ends up on a square occupied by an opposing piece or pawn, it captures that piece or pawn.

Pawn (P): On its first move, a pawn may advance straight ahead one or two squares. On other moves, it can move straight ahead one square at a time, or move ahead diagonally to capture an enemy piece or pawn.

Rook (R): A rook can move along any rank or file until it meets another piece or pawn. It can stop on the square of an enemy piece or pawn, capturing it.

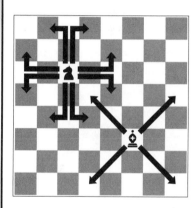

Knight (N): A knight moves two squares on any rank or file and then one square to the left or to the right. If it lands on an enemy piece or pawn, it captures it. A knight is the only piece that can leap over another piece.

Bishop (B): A bishop moves on a diagonal until it meets another piece or pawn. It can stop on the square of an enemy piece or pawn, capturing it.

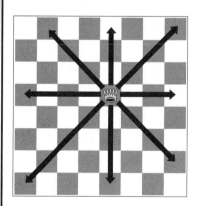

Queen (Q): The queen moves on any diagonal, rank, or file until it meets another piece or pawn. It can stop on the square of an enemy piece or pawn, capturing it.

Once a game, each player can make a two-part move called "castling," to protect the king. It's permitted if the king has not yet moved and if there are no pieces between the king and a rook. For example, when white castles "queenside," the king moves to c1 and the rook moves to d1. In "kingside" castling, the king moves to g1 and the rook to f1.

SAMPLE GAME

Paul Morphy is known as the "father of modern chess." Every chess master has studied his games. In this game, which took place in Paris in 1858, Morphy plays the White pieces against the team of Count Isouard and the Duke of Brunswick.

In the list of moves, White's moves are given first followed by a comma, and then Black's moves except when I make a comment.

If no piece is named, the move involves a pawn. Thus, "c6" means that a pawn moves to the square c6.

1. e4

White (Morphy) begins by moving a pawn to e4. At the start of a game, the long-range pieces (bishop, queen, rook) can't take part in an attack because they are blocked by the row of pawns. White's move makes room for his bishop and queen to enter the action.

1. ...e5

Black's move is to e5.

2. Nf3, d6
3. d4

A good chess player is aware of all threats to capture. On move 2, White threatened to take the unprotected pawn on e5. Now the same threat appears again, since there are two attackers of e5 and only one defender.

3. ...Bg4
4. dxe5, Bxf3

The "x" symbol means capture. In this case, White's pawn captures Black's pawn on e5, then Black's bishop captures White's knight on f3.

5. Qxf3, dxe5
6. Bc4

White has two long-range pieces in action, controlling the center of the board and threatening checkmate—the end of the game. "Checkmate" happens when the king can't escape. Capturing on f7 with the queen would be checkmate. Learn to recognize checkmate patterns.

6. ...Nf6
7. Qb3

Good chess players work with double threats. Here, White threatens the unprotected pawn on b7, and also checkmate in two moves on f7.

7. ...Qe7

8. Nc3

Why doesn't Morphy capture the b7 pawn? Only because he won't have enough attacking pieces.

8. ...c6

9. Bg5

The Black knight on f6 is "pinned" to the queen—if the knight moves, the queen will be taken.

9. ...b5

10. Nxb5, cxb5

Black's pawn captures White's knight. Morphy knew that a knight is more valuable than two pawns, but he sacrificed it to get at the Black king. Black's bishop on f8 and rook on h8 are out of play, and can't save the king.

11. Bxb5+, Nbd7

The + sign means "check"—a warning that the other player's king is in immediate risk of being taken. It is illegal to remain in check.

12. 0-0-0

0-0-0 means that White has castled "queenside." The symbol for "kingside" castling is 0-0.

12. ...Rd8

13. Rxd7, Rxd7

14. Rd1

White brings in his last reserve rook. Notice that Black (the Count and the Duke) will have a problem bringing in their last reserve rook.

14. ...Qe6

15. Bxd7+, Nxd7

If White could get his rook to d8 it would be checkmate!

16. Qb8+, Nxb8

17. Rd8#

The # signals checkmate: the king has been caught. The game is over. Note how White's two pieces combined in this checkmate. Black's pieces are scattered and useless. The bishop and rook are on their original squares, unmoved. The knight had come out and gone back home. The king never got castled. The queen looks aimlessly about.

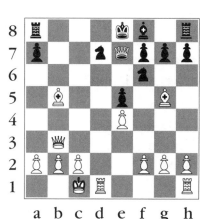

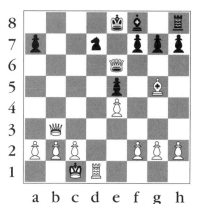

Peter Kurzdorfer is a National Chess Master. He teaches chess workshops and offers an interactive chess course. He is also the assistant editor of *Chess Life* magazine. You can reach him via e-mail at cheslife@warwick.net.

HOW TO Plan an Unforgettable

—by Pamela Beck

My passion for throwing parties began when I was 11. I was seeking an adventure of my own design, mixing friends, food, and dance music. Over the years, it's become a creative challenge, like directing a play. The surprise is—hosting a party can be easy. All you need is an interesting blend of people, careful preparation, and attention to detail. You are cordially invited to use any of my party-planning tips.

DIRECTIONS

1. Find a reason to bring people together.

Besides birthdays and the usual holidays, you can throw a party just for the fun of it. Be inventive. Check out the calendar for holidays that other countries celebrate. The library is a gold mine of ideas. Spend some time there researching themes. Research will provide you with the kind of details that will make your parties unique and memorable.

2. Plan the event. Many parties focus on conversation and food. But a get-together can be an excuse for enjoying all sorts of experiences. A theme party can introduce you and your guests to new foods, clothing, decor, games, music, dances, and customs. This could work for a Roaring 20s party, a Hawaiian Luau, a Japanese Tea Ceremony, a Johnny Appleseed Day party, or a come-as-your-favorite-cartoon-character party. Here are some suggestions for activities:

• Have an expert teach a skill, such as juggling, magic tricks, kite making, or sand-sculpting.
• Involve guests in the food preparation, for example, by adding toppings to pizzas.
• Arrange for a performance by a local band or theater group.
• Write a skit and have guests play the parts. *continued* . . .

3. Draw up your guest list. Whether you're inviting dozens of friends or just a few, give your list careful thought. Who would make an interesting group? Don't worry about only inviting people who know each other. It's fun to meet new people.

4. Schedule the event. Check your calendar to make sure you won't be competing with a holiday (like Mother's Day) or a major event (like a football championship game). If you're planning an outdoors party, have a back-up plan in case the weather doesn't cooperate.

5. Design the invitations. Although it's easy to buy invitations, you can explore your creative side by making your own. If your party includes dancing, you might make the invitations look like CDs. If you're giving a party for a practical joker, slip one of those hand-buzzer gags into each envelope.

Be sure to list all the important details on the invitation: time, date, location, necessary clothing or gear (swimsuit, hiking boots, rollerblades, etc.), and R.S.V.P. information. (The letters R.S.V.P. are derived from the French phrase *repondez-vous s'il vous plait*, which means "Please reply.")

6. Mail invitations one month ahead of time. That way your guests will have plenty of notice.

7. Keep track of responses. If you don't hear from someone, phone the person to make sure the invitation arrived. If too many people are unable to attend, there's no shame in changing the date.

8. Plan the menu. If you're having a theme party, design your menu around your theme. Have enough choices so that if someone is a vegetarian or has a particular food allergy, there is an alternative. Serve dishes that you can prepare in advance so that during the party you can relax and have a good time. And if you're thinking of trying out a new recipe, test it on your family first, just in case.

continued ...

9. Think about how the food will be served. If you have a sit-down meal, ask an older sibling or your parents to help serve. Otherwise, try a buffet. Buffets can be fun for desserts, potlucks, and outdoor BBQs. They're also good for build-your-own sandwich parties! Make things look attractive. They'll always taste better that way.

10. On the day of the party, prepare more food than you think you'll need. One of the surest ways to ruin a party and feel embarrassed is to run out of food!

11. Decorate your party location. Let your imagination take you beyond traditional decorations. If you're throwing a goodbye party for someone taking a trip, put up a map showing the person's destination. For an anniversary party, make a giant blow-up of the couple on their wedding day.

In addition to decorations, remember to put away any valuable items that might break.

12. Introduce guests who don't know each other. Some people are shy and won't introduce themselves to a stranger. It's up to you to make sure everybody is mingling and having fun. There will always be some common ground between your guests—where they live, sports, hobbies and interests, who they know, and so on.

If you're having a sit-down dinner, arrange for people who don't know each other to sit together. Do this by putting place cards around the table designating who sits where. For additional fun, after the main course, have people change seats so they can talk to someone different during dessert.

Pamela Beck is a best-selling novelist, a screenwriter, and the co-founder of Double Whammy Productions, a film and TV company. She has thrown nearly 1,000 parties in her lifetime.

A final tip: Be sure to enjoy the party yourself! When guests see you having fun, they relax and have a better time themselves. And remember, your party will be over way too fast. So take plenty of pictures!

PART 4

HOW TO Do Well in School

—by Tamina Stephenson

Doing well in school is no different from doing well at playing the piano, hitting a baseball, or painting. It takes discipline, practice, and determination. Having brains helps, too. Let's face it: some people are naturally faster at picking things up than others.

However, all of us are intelligent beings whether we know it or not. We speak intricate languages; we live in societies so complex that college professors keep on trying to figure them out; and we use ingenious tools every day. (Think how many pieces it takes to make a pencil sharpener.) So even if you don't think you're smart, if you are a human being, you *are*.

The skills and habits you pick up early in school can help you later on, but you don't need to have walked home from your first day of kindergarten with gold stars to get a good grade point average in middle school or high school. Doing well in school can begin whenever you're ready. In my last 12 years as a student, I've picked up a few strategies that I hope will help you.

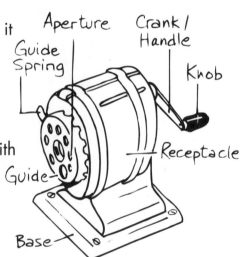

Aperture
Crank / Handle
Guide Spring
Knob
Guide
Receptacle
Base

DIRECTIONS

1. Pay attention. This may sound simple and obvious, but it's a major key to doing well in school. When a teacher is explaining something, listen carefully. Try to catch every word so that you can filter them and extract the important information. It often helps to look at teachers when they talk. If possible, sit near the front of the room. Think of the way fortunetellers sit close to the person whose future they are trying to see. When you learn, in a way you are trying to read your teacher's mind.

A fish's gills...

continued ...

2. If you don't understand something the first time, don't worry. Worrying just closes the mind like a tense muscle, making it hard to think. This, of course, is the last thing you want.

3. Ask questions to clarify what's confusing you. If you are having a hard time even figuring out what to ask, just try to open your brain to it and listen to the general idea. You should also listen carefully to other people's questions and answers, because they can clear things up or help you frame your own questions. Often ideas that are confusing one day have a way of sorting themselves while you sleep that night, and will be much clearer in the morning.

If you are still totally baffled about something the second or third time it comes up, then it's time to take action. Just raise your hand and say you don't get it—you're probably not the only one. A good teacher will usually try to explain it in a different way or go at it from a different angle, which nearly always helps.

4. If you need to, stay after class and ask the teacher for help individually. Eventually, you *will* understand. After all, there was a time when using a spoon or drinking out of a cup seemed complicated, but we all become experts at it well before we tackle long division.

Grasping ideas is the first half of the school battle. The second half, especially once you get into the upper grades and beyond, is handling the work. When you get old enough that teachers begin to assign serious homework and long-term projects, the key to success (and sanity) is organization.

continued ...

5. Write down your assignments. Whether it's nightly homework or a twenty-page report, write the assignment down, with its due date, where you won't lose it. Some people like to use calendars or weekly planners. In this case, it is often a good idea to write occasional reminders. For instance, if a report is due in two weeks, write something like *remember report* a week before the due date.

Rather than using a calendar, I prefer to make a list of all my assignments in a small memo pad, so that I can scan through everything quickly. When I finish something, I cross it out. You'll see an example of one of my lists in the margin.

When I have a major assignment, I write down its requirements, such as length or format, somewhere else so that I don't bog down my list with extra information. Usually I put these specifics with my other work from that class.

6. Follow through. There is no point writing down four reminders to yourself to start a big paper if you still don't get around to it until the night before it's due. Sometimes people can do very good jobs throwing things together at the last minute, but it's always better to pace yourself.

Let's say you have to turn in a report three weeks from now. Go to the library and check out books now, even if you don't have time to start looking in them right away. Then you can start finding information from the books in your spare moments. Before you actually start writing your report, try to find the time to give it some thought; make a rough plan in your head. When you sit down with your pen or keyboard, it helps immensely to have some idea of where to begin. This way, even if you do end up doing a lot of work at the last minute, it will already have had a start. Sometimes starting is the hardest part.

continued ...

> ### ASSIGNMENTS
> <u>Math</u>: page 21 (#15 - 23, 30 - 33) due Wed.
> <u>English</u>: read Chapters 1 & 2 by Tues.
> <u>Drama</u>: memorize lines by Thurs. 4/24.
> <u>History</u>: Civil War essay due Mon. 4/21.
> <u>Chemistry</u>: test Fri. on Chapters 6 - 8.

7. Enjoy life. If you are bothering to read this, you probably agree with me that school is important. Remember, though, that it isn't everything. Whether you are a third-grader or a graduate student, you need to have balance in your life. You should make sure you devote some time each week to things you enjoy and that are fulfilling to you—practicing an instrument, reading, playing sports, or whatever it is you like to do. Schoolwork gets old really fast if you don't take time off to relax.

Weekends are great for helping achieve this balance. If you get little or no homework over the weekend, then you can work hard all week knowing that you'll be able to kick back for a couple of days. If you're not so lucky, however, don't despair. As a high school student, I sometimes have to do a lot of homework over the weekend, so I make a point of not working straight through. For instance, if I'm home on a Friday afternoon I might do homework only if I have plans for the evening. On the other hand, if I hang out with my friends until 6 p.m., then I'll be refreshed enough to go home and get a bit of work done. The same idea applies to Saturdays: work some, play some. Because I spend so much time on homework, I often devote almost all of Sunday to it, but at least I've usually had some fun during the previous day or two.

I hope my advice on learning, working, and balancing your life will help you a bit. It would take a much longer article—a few books and then some—to solve every problem we ever encounter in school, but at least these few tips might make your way a little bit smoother.

Oh, and by the way, if you ever find that "much longer article," be sure to tell me about it. I could sure use it.

Tamina Stephenson wrote this as a senior (Class of '98) at Sir Francis Drake High School in San Anselmo, California. Besides earning a GPA above 4.0, she has been involved with Drake's theater company, newspaper, and literary magazine. She is also the first student in the school's history to score a perfect 1600 on the SAT.

HOW TO Write a Report

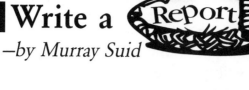

—by Murray Suid

The word *report* literally means "to carry back." The report maker goes on a search for knowledge, and later carries it back to share with others.

DIRECTIONS

1. Focus your topic. You can find countless facts on almost every topic. You can't collect them all. But a question can narrow the range. For example, a report on pigs might focus on one of the following questions:

- Are pigs really dirty?
- How are pigs different from other animals?
- Do pigs make good pets?

If you can't think of a question, read a book or an article on the topic. This kind of "background reading" can stimulate questions.

2. Look for information to answer your question. Three ways to gather information are:

- Using books, videos, Web sites, and other media.
- Talking to experts face to face, by phone, or by mail.
- Observing the subject firsthand.

3. Collect the facts. Don't write information that you already know, such as, "Pigs have four legs." List facts that are new to you, for example, "The pig is related to the hippopotamus."

- To better understand the material, paraphrase it. This means putting it into your own words.
- To make it easier to organize your facts, try using note cards. Put one fact on a card. Add the source of the fact and any thoughts that you have about it.

continued ...

HOW TO PARAPHRASE

- Read a passage carefully.
- Put it aside. Don't look at it.
- Think about it.
- Write the information in your own words. Use language that you understand.
- Reread the original passage to make sure that you captured the important facts and ideas. While looking at the passage, it's OK to copy details such as dates, names, and numbers.

4. Check your information. Try to find a second source for each fact. If two sources disagree, find a third. Ask yourself if the person who presented the information is a real expert.

5. Draft your report. Present the facts clearly and concisely. If you're writing a formal report, you may need to include notes that tell where you found each important fact. You can do this by placing a number near each fact and then giving information about it at the bottom of the page or on a separate page.

6. Add illustrations that give useful information. These can be original drawings or photographs.

7. Test the report. Ask someone to read it. Then discuss the ideas with your trial reader to see if the person understands what you wrote.

8. Polish the report. Change it according to the comments you received from your trial reader. Check all spelling and punctuation.

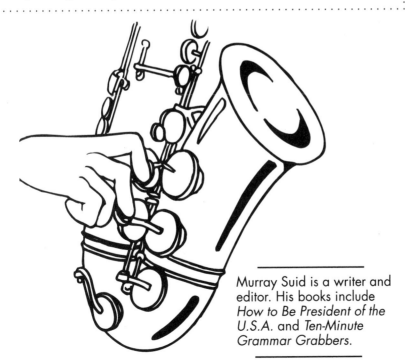

Murray Suid is a writer and editor. His books include *How to Be President of the U.S.A.* and *Ten-Minute Grammar Grabbers.*

SAMPLE REPORT

The Easy-to-Play Woodwind

Although made of brass, the saxophone is classified as a woodwind instrument. Other woodwinds include the oboe and the clarinet.[1]

Antoine Sax invented and named the instrument in the 1840s. The second syllable "phone" is from a Greek word meaning "sound."[2]

To play notes on a saxophone, the saxophonist presses padded keys.[3] A clarinetist, on the other hand, covers most of the holes using the fingers. This makes the clarinet harder to play.[4]

Notes
1. *The Concise Columbia Encyclopedia* (Avon, 1983, p. 924).
2. *Webster's New World Dictionary* (Collins, 1974, p. 1070).
3. *Word People* by Nancy Sorel (American Heritage, 1970, p. 253).
4. Personal observation.

HOW TO Explore The Past

—by Mary Lowenthal Felstiner

I became a historian in the fifth grade. I was fascinated by the sea voyages of Spanish explorers like Vasco da Gama, Ponce de León, and Ferdinand Magellan. In most ways, they were different from me. Yet by learning about them, I also learned about myself. For example, I found it comforting that figures who accomplished great deeds started small. Watching them grow helped me prepare for my own future.

If you want to visit the past, read history books. More exciting, become a historian yourself. You don't need a time machine. All it takes is curiosity, research skills, and imagination.

DIRECTIONS

1. Get interested in a person. Just one individual can become the subject of your historical research. Your subject can be someone you know— for example, a relative or a neighbor. Or it can be a figure you have heard of. If you ask yourself about the person's life, you will also find yourself learning about the period when the person lived.

2. Don't focus too much on specific dates. Instead, think about larger chunks of time in which the person lived: Think about decades and even centuries. For example, if you're writing about someone who lived in the nineteenth century, you'll know immediately that the person didn't watch TV. But what did they do in those days for amusement or to get the news? And did "news" have the same meaning for your subject as it does for you?

continued ...

3. Pay attention to changes in the subject's life. Did the person move from one city to another or take up a hobby? Ask why. Much of history is about noticing and explaining small changes. Here are two ways to practice observing change:

• As you walk down a street, be aware of differences. Has a store gone out of business? Did someone repaint a house? What do you think makes change happen in a neighborhood?

• When watching an old movie, look for differences in clothes, jobs, songs, or jokes between its time and the present. What's changed most and why? If it's a new movie, how might the same story have been told in your grandparents' time?

4. Do research to find information. You might look in diaries, letters, and old newspapers. You might interview people who knew your subject. In some cases you may have to guess at the answer; this is called making a hypothesis. But even if you can't know everything for certain, by asking questions and searching for facts, you're doing real research.

5. Analyze what shaped the life of your subject. Were there big forces, such as prejudice or a war? What role did education play? Did the person read a book that changed his or her life? Did anyone point your subject in a new direction?

6. Recreate the past. As you learn about your subject's life and environment, use your imagination to put yourself there. Try to see yourself doing everyday activities just the way the person did.

7. Share your knowledge. Try writing an essay or a story about your subject's life. Remember that what you see as the past was the subject's present or future, something the person was just learning about.

Mary Lowenthal Felstiner is a professor of history at San Francisco State University. She is the author of *To Paint Her Life: Charlotte Salomon in the Nazi Era.*

HOW TO Give a Speech

—by Wanda Lincoln

You can learn to love speaking in public. It all starts with the right attitude. Look at the title of this article. The key word is "Give." If you think of your speech as a gift, the audience will more likely enjoy your presentation, and so will you.

DIRECTIONS

1. Have a clear purpose. A speech can give information, present an opinion, teach a skill, or move people to action. Some speeches have more than one purpose, but it's best to concentrate on a single goal. Another way to think about purpose is to ask yourself: What one thing do I want the audience to remember or do after I sit down?

2. Know your audience. Just as it's important to match a gift to the recipient, you need to match your speech to the people who will receive it. For example, if you're explaining bike racing to people who have never done it, you'll need to explain the basics. On the other hand, if you're talking to experienced bike racers, you would cover more advanced material.

3. Research your topic. Often, you will need to add to your knowledge. Research is vital because audiences enjoy a speech that contains interesting material they never knew before. This step includes collecting materials that you will present, for example, pictures, artifacts, and recordings.

continued ...

Isosceles triangles also...

4. Draft the speech. Writing your speech will help you clarify your ideas, get the timing right, and gain confidence. There are four parts to work on:

• *Title*: Create an original title. It can be used by the person introducing you. Note: If you're introducing yourself, be brief.

• *Opening "hook"*: Grab attention fast. You might show a cartoon, give an amazing fact, or toss out a challenge: "In the next 30 minutes, I'm going to teach everyone here how to juggle."

• *Body*: Organize your ideas in a way that is easy for the audience to follow, such as chronological order or as a list of points from least important to most important. Use clear language, avoid over-long sentences, and include examples. Also, plan strategies to keep people interested. You might present an object related to the topic or ask the audience to try a quick activity.

• *Closing*: Keep it short. Avoid weak endings like "Well, I guess that's all I have to say." Instead, find a powerful way to conclude the speech. It might be your most important fact, a quotation by a famous person, or a call to action: "Now, I hope you will start recycling today! Thank you."

5. Rehearse by yourself. Practice the speech several times until you're confident. It's best if you can deliver it without reading the words. Although you should memorize your opening and closing, for the rest of your speech know the ideas so well you can talk from your heart. If necessary, write a few notes to help you recall the key points. Also:

• Be sure you correctly pronounce all the words.

• Work on your entrance, posture, gestures, and facial expressions. Don't fidget.

• If using audio or visual aids, practice handling them and any equipment. Be sure visuals are large enough to be seen or read at the back of the room.

• Time your speech. If you are scheduled to give a five-minute talk, don't ramble on for ten minutes.

continued ...

6. Practice with a trial audience. Go all the way through the speech without stopping. Pay special attention to eye contact. After finishing, discuss each section of the speech, and try it again. If you plan to answer questions during the actual presentation, practice doing so with your trial audience.

7. On the day of the speech, prepare yourself. Little details can make a big difference:
• Wear an outfit that you feel comfortable in and that projects a positive image. Avoid distracting items.
• Take along a mint for possible dry mouth and a tissue for sweaty palms.
• Arrive at the location in plenty of time. If it's a place you've never spoken in before—for example, an auditorium—walk around the room to familiarize yourself with it.

8. Give the speech. Remember: You are giving a gift. After you make your entrance:
• Get set for a moment before opening your mouth.
• Deliver your opening boldly.
• Look for friendly faces in the audience. Most people will be rooting for you to do well. There are always a few people, even total strangers, who will encourage you with smiles and nods of approval. At all costs: avoid giving your attention to people who seem uninterested.

9. Later, think about your presentation. Give yourself credit for the things you did well, and review the parts that you'd like to improve. This kind of self-evaluation, which is done by athletes, musicians, actors, and all other performers, is the secret to improving your skills.

BEAT STAGE FRIGHT

Almost everyone is nervous before speaking. This nervousness is just energy. Instead of letting it control you, you can control and use it to do a better job!

Ahead of Time

• *Get used to having people focus on you.* When you speak, the audience's attention is on you. This can make you feel strange. The remedy is to practice being in that situation. Stand in front of a group of friends. Say nothing. Just watch them watching you. Soon you will see that there is nothing to fear in being stared at.

• *Play charades or other performance games.* The more experience you get in front of people, the more relaxed you'll feel speaking.

• *Prepare easy-to-read notes.* Nerves can make you forget an important idea. If you get lost, look at your notes and you'll be able to get back on track.

• *Plan a sure-fire beginning.* It may help to start with an activity that involves the audience and lets you relax. Try reading to the audience, giving them a quiz, or asking them to do an experiment.

• *Anticipate problems.* Know what you'll do if the projector doesn't work, or if you drop your notes, or if people don't laugh at your funniest line. Preparing for problems will make you feel more confident.

• *Be sure you have given yourself adequate practice.*

Right Before Giving Your Speech

• *Meet members of the audience.* This will remind you that public speaking is simply talking to other people.

• *If you feel a lot of nervous energy, do a physical exercise.* Walk around. Stretch. Jog in place.

• *Give yourself a pep talk.* Remind yourself that you have worked hard on the speech and that you know the subject.

• *Visualize yourself successfully giving the speech.* This is what many athletes do before going into competition.

• *Smile as you make your entrance.* By instinct, people will smile back, and you'll feel their positive energy.

Wanda Lincoln is a teacher. She has been a workshop leader for more than 20 years, and has given hundreds of speeches around the world.

HOW TO Get Good at M+a+t+h

—by Margo Nanny

One day when I was 10 and riding home from school, I noticed a sign on the bus: "Count the change in your pocket." (I counted 35 cents.) "Now," said the sign, "double that." (70) "Add 20." (70 + 20 = 90) "Divide by 2." (45) "Subtract 10." (35) "And that," said the sign, "is how much change you have in your pocket!"

Wait a minute! How could the sign know how much change I had in my pocket? I did it again. And again it knew. I put 15 cents in my other pocket and did it with that amount. It still knew. I didn't get it.

I went home and played with the problem all weekend. It was fascinating. I drew pictures, including a picture of an empty box to represent any amount of change that was in a person's pocket. I eventually discovered that you could take any number, do some arithmetic on it, undo the arithmetic, and get the number you started with. I decided that the problem was equivalent to this: "Pick any number. Add 10. Subtract 10." Wowee, zowee, you've got your number. Nothing to it.

When the sign said "Double it, add 20, divide by 2, subtract 10," it didn't seem so simple. But really it's the same thing. Years later, I realized that to solve this problem, I had invented my own algebra. The box was the same as the symbol X (for the unknown). Only then did I realize that this was the experience that started me on the path of exploring mathematical things.

This story teaches that mathematics isn't just about getting a right answer. It involves getting involved with a problem, sticking with it, drawing pictures, experimenting, and even having fun. The more you work at it, the better you'll get.

COIN PROBLEM

To get good at math you need good problems. You can find them in many library books and on the Internet. For now, here is one of my favorites.

A mathemagical troll jumps from your closet and offers you one of his 12 gold coins. The only trouble: 11 are fake. The real coin is heavier than the fakes. The troll offers you his balance scale to find the real coin, but you can use it only three times before the scale turns into a frog. Can you find the gold coin in three weighings?

The answer appears in the box on the next page. But don't look at it until you work on the problem yourself.

DIRECTIONS

1. When problem solving, expect to be confused. Don't worry if you come up with wrong solutions; it's part of doing math and happens to the most brilliant mathematicians. A "wrong" answer often leads to the solution you are after.

2. If you're stuck, look at the problem from other angles. Try a guess and check it out. Draw pictures and diagrams to help you visualize. Restate the problem in your own words. Make up a simple version of the problem. If you can solve that one, use your method on the original problem.

3. If it's a complicated word problem, avoid calculating as long as possible. Figure out a possible solution before applying an algorithm. For example, don't start multiplying and carrying numbers until you know where you're going.

4. Ask yourself questions. Keep asking. Use the questions as starting points for experiments.

5. Find a buddy to work with. Math at times is a social activity. It's OK to talk to someone about a problem when you're stuck. Don't ask the person to do all the work for you. Instead, talk about what you've tried so far to solve the problem. The other person might give you a hint that will point you in the right direction.

6. When you finally do get it, play with it. Don't stop just because you have the right answer. Make up more interesting problems than they have in the book. Think up weird uses of the problem.

7. Don't get behind on your homework. Math needs to sink in a little at a time. Playing catchup can overload your brain.

COIN PROBLEM SOLUTION

1. Place all 12 coins on the scale—6 coins on the left and six coins on the right:

xxxxxx   xxxxxx

The group with the heavier (gold) coin will move down. In this example, it's the group on the right:

xxxxxx

2. Place the heavier group on the scale, 3 coins on each side, and see which group is heavier. In this example, it's heavier on the left:

xxx
xxx

3. Take the heavier group, and place 2 of the coins on the scale. Put the third coin off to one side:

x   x   x

• If one coin on the scale weighs more than the other, that's your gold coin. • If the coins on the scale weigh the same, you know by the process of elimination that the third coin must be made of gold.

Margo Nanny has taught kids and adults math and math-related things like carpentry. For the past 10 years Margo has been creating educational CD-Rom games, such as *Countdown*, *Planetary Taxi*, and *Top Secret Decoder*.

HOW TO Be a Better Reader

—by Sue Krumbein

With planning and perseverance, you can improve your reading skills, and enjoy doing so. Review the following strategies. Then begin anywhere. It's not important to go in order. What matters is that you do something, keep at it, and then try something else. Good luck and have fun!

DIRECTIONS

1. Spend time in the library. In a library, you're surrounded by reading materials and readers. What better place to be? If you already have a library card, good. If not, sign up for one. It's almost always free. On your own or with the help of a librarian, explore:

• *The new book section.* New books are such a pleasure. They're crisp and clean, and their covers are so appealing.

• *The fiction section.* As you browse, choose several books to check out. This way you're more likely to have at least one that pleases you. Try books recommended by friends. Also, if you like a book by a certain author, there's a good chance you'll like other books by the same person.

• *The nonfiction section.* Whatever your interests—animals, camping, computers, juggling, photography—you can almost always find a factual book on that topic. A bonus with nonfiction is that you can read a chapter and enjoy it; you don't have to read the whole book.

• *Book displays.* Librarians often set up topical displays. Take a look; something might interest you.

• *Magazines and newspapers.* These contain a wide variety of short pieces on every subject imaginable. Browse to see what you like and then ask if you can check out back issues.

continued ...

2. Schedule at least two reading times a day. It's important to read regularly to improve. Many good readers read for 15 to 30 minutes before bedtime. You might also read while: eating a snack, using public transportation, waiting for an activity to begin, or relaxing after an activity or strenuous exercise. Try following a set reading schedule for two weeks to develop a reading habit.

3. Find a reading partner. Ask the person to read the same book you're reading. Then discuss it. If you have a pen pal or e-mail pal, comment on what you're reading.

4. Check out your local bookstores. Owning even a few books will remind you that you care about reading. To save money, try browsing in a store that sells used books.

5. Put books on your gift list. This lets your family and friends know that you are a reader.

6. Think about what you read. If a book interests you, look for another on that subject.

7. View yourself as a reader. A positive attitude is vital in developing skills in sports, science, art—and reading. Believing you are a reader will make you more open to reading.

SELECTING A BOOK

How can you choose from the vast number of books in a library or bookstore? Here are some guidelines:

• Make a list of topics that interest you: skateboarding, TV comedy, football. Look up these subjects to see what books are available.

• Think of an author or two whose writing you have enjoyed. Check to see what else the person has written, or ask the librarian for some comparable authors.

• Check out the sorting shelf at the library. These are books that have just been returned, which someone else might have enjoyed.

• Get to know the librarian, whose job is to help you. Most librarians are avid readers and like to make suggestions.

Sue Krumbein is a librarian in Menlo Park, California. Before becoming a librarian, she was an English teacher. Her favorite authors include Barbara Kingsolver and Margaret Atwood.

HOW TO Create a Science Fair Project

—by Nick Kallen

A science fair project can be one of the most exciting and engaging activities in your school career. Unfortunately, it can also be one of the most excessive bores. The following guidelines may help to keep your science fair project fun and successful.

DIRECTIONS

1. Choose your project carefully. When selecting something to study, consider three questions:

• *Does this topic really interest you?* If not, you won't enjoy much of your science fair experience. My successful projects have grown from important historical experiments. Other sources of topics include what you're studying in science class or what you observe on your own.

• *Is the research doable?* If you select a project that you cannot actually accomplish, you will doom yourself to frustration. To decide if you can actually accomplish a project, you must consider issues such as: the cost of the materials, the mental and physical skills required, and the amount of time the investigation will take.

• *Is it appropriate?* If you select a project that is inappropriate for a science fair, a bad grade can be the only result. Judging appropriateness can be extremely hard, especially since certain projects blur the line between different sciences. Consult your teachers frequently when uncertain about these things.

continued ...

2. Plan to revise. It is often the case, especially in more competitive science fairs, that winning projects are revisions of projects done in previous years. If your science fair is competitive, you must take this into consideration. That means intending from the start to revise your project for the next fair. When choosing a topic, be sure that it is one you can add to and revise in the future.

3. Know the four elements of a project:

• *Research*. Discovering or analyzing data (numbers that come from experiments) is at the heart of every successful project. Your data, of course, must be for a purpose, such as: to prove a theory, to measure a value, or to predict future events. Hint: Attempt your project promptly and do not become frustrated with early failures—they will lead you to success.

• *Notebook*. One of the key presentation materials is a project notebook. Start building your notebook from the first day you begin a science fair project. Date every page and include in chronological order every thought, idea, and attempt you make. Not only will this help you to be successful with the judges, but it will aid you in being more organized.

• *Presentation board*. You will create the presentation board after your research is finished. The purpose of this free-standing display is to efficiently convey information that aids you in your oral presentation. Specifically, it will present: the project outline, data and statistical diagrams, hypotheses, conclusions, plus other requirements of the specific science fair.

• *The oral presentation*. Carefully plan and rehearse what you want to say. During the presentation, be confident. You should concisely illustrate (with the aid of your presentation board) what your project is, how it works, why it is significant, and what conclusions should be drawn from it. It is vital that you come off as understanding your project.

Nick Kallen won first place for physics in the 1996 Los Angeles County Science Fair. His project, entitled "Finding the Universal Gravitational Constant," also took fourth place in the California State Science Fair.

If you dedicate yourself and follow the above guidelines, you should be able to enjoy yourself and create a project that can successfully compete in your science fair.

HOW TO Edit a Manuscript
—by Terry Walton

I'm a professional editor. I improve what other people write. This job involves finding ways to make a manuscript clearer, more accurate, and more readable. By learning how to edit, you can help your friends with their writing. You can even edit your own work. Along the way, you'll improve your grammar, vocabulary, and other writing skills.

DIRECTIONS

1. If the writing is yours, put it aside. This will help you approach the words with a fresh eye.

2. Make sure the manuscript is typed double-spaced and has wide margins. You need room to make corrections and to give suggestions.

3. Set up your editing area. I prefer an uncluttered table in a quiet place. My tools are: a good eraser and an 0.5 lead mechanical pencil.

4. Read the text first without making notes. You need to get the big picture before figuring out changes.

5. Use standard editing symbols. Even if you're working on your own writing, the marks will be valuable when you begin entering the changes.

6. Delete weak words and trite phrases. If a word's meaning or spelling seems wrong, mark it and look it up.

7. Make notes in the margins. Point out unclear ideas or statements that don't seem true.

8. When done, put the manuscript away. Come back to it later for final polishing. It's a peaceful end to a pleasing task.

EDITING MARKS

- **Capitalize.**

  australia = Australia

- **Use lower case.**

  I Laugh. = I laugh.

- **Delete (remove).**

  I do see. = I see.

- **Delete and replace.**

  easy
  It's quick. = It's easy.

- **Insert text.**

  jmp = jump

- **Insert a mark.**

  It works = It works.

- **Insert a space.**

  Wakeup. = Wake up.

- **Move together.**

  until = until

- **Move text.**

  I sad am. = I am sad.

- **Begin a paragraph.**

  ¶

Terry Walton is a free-lance editor and writer from Cold Spring Harbor, Long Island. She has edited books and newsletters on many topics including computers, sailing, and architecture.

PART 5

SELF-IMPROVEMENT

HOW TO Be More Tolerant

—by Ruth Schwartz

Have you ever put someone down because of color, religion, or ethnic background? Have you ever avoided someone because the person was disabled? I've heard many people share their pain and sadness when they have been made fun of or excluded because they are different in some way. This is the type of story I have heard:

> I was both happy and scared when I started my new school. It was a nicer school than my old one, but I didn't know anyone. When I was taken to my classroom, I saw that no one else was my color or from the country my family was from. The teacher asked if someone would volunteer to be with me at recess and lunchtime. No one raised a hand. A few even laughed.
>
> I've been at my school for three weeks. I'm the last picked for a team, even though I play better than a lot of the kids. I eat lunch alone. A couple of kids have told me, "Go back where you came from." A few kids feel sorry for me, but their friends make fun of them if they start to be friendly. I hate my school, and I'm even beginning to hate myself!

Can you step into that person's shoes and share the feelings of hurt? If you will honestly try, you have opened the door to becoming more tolerant. On the next page, you'll find five more suggestions.

SUGGESTIONS

1. Judge each person as an individual. Do not think of all people of the same race or religion as being the same. There are good and bad people in every group.

2. Do not be fearful of people who are different from you. Learn to know and understand the other person and appreciate the differences. You'll grow into a more interesting person as you expand your world.

3. Be responsibe for your weaknesses. Work to improve yourself a little at a time. Do not use other groups as an excuse for the problems in your life.

4. Do not blame a whole group for the crimes or faults of a few in that group. Do you remember when 168 people were killed in the bombing of the federal building in Oklahoma? Many people quickly blamed foreign terrorists from one part of the world, and even sent hate letters to people of the same background. The criminal turned out to be a white American. Does that mean we should hate every Caucasian? Of course not! The lesson is: We should reject the notion of collective guilt.

5. Work on positive ways to improve yourself. Do not try to build yourself up by putting others down. A person with good self-esteem doesn't need to demonstrate superiority over anyone.

You have the power to love or to hate. You can choose to reach your potential or to allow intolerance to limit your growth as a human being. Could you have made a difference in the life of the child in that story?

Ruth Schwartz volunteers as a docent in the Museum of Tolerance, Los Angeles, California. The museum is devoted to promoting tolerance and understanding.

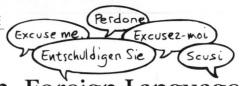

HOW TO Learn a Foreign Language
—by Ronald Kruschak

I remember my first English lesson. I was a 12-year-old German schoolboy. My teacher, Frau Schmidt, looked at me and said, "We can't call you *Ronald* in this class. *Ronald* is not a name that people use in Great Britain or America."

Apparently, Frau Schmidt had never heard of Ronald Reagan, who at that time was a well-known actor. Nor had she heard of Ronald McDonald or other famous Ronalds.

So I became *Ron*, and Frau Schmidt began teaching me and my friends what *Peter* and *Mary* did in their *house* with their *dog* and *cat* and *bird*. This was not the most exciting stuff in the world. I soon realized that I had to look for a new way of learning English. The answer was to study the lyrics of pop music. If you like music and want to learn a language, here's how to do it.

DIRECTIONS
1. Find a group that sings in the language you want to learn.
In my case, it was the Beatles. These were teachers I could respect. They gave me a real perspective for my life as hundreds of breathtakingly pretty girls chased them through a fabulous, adventurous movie, *A Hard Day's Night.*

2. Listen to songs over and over until you master the words.
This is the kind of assignment Frau Schmidt never gave. But I didn't need her to push me. I practically wore out a Beatles' tape learning English. Because I didn't have the cover with the printed lyrics, I had to figure out the song titles myself. One of my favorites was "Can Bummy Love?"

continued ...

3. Think about the meaning of each song.

"Can Bummy Love?" made me feel part of the grown-up world for the first time. I wondered, "Is it *that* difficult to love?" If the Beatles didn't know whether this guy "Bummy" could love, how could I ever expect to be able to love? Would I end up sad and lonely like old Bummy? I felt for Bummy. Bummy was my friend.

4. Be humble.
Finally, the day came when I discovered that "Can Bummy Love?" was actually "Can't Buy Me Love." There was no Bummy. And I felt like a dummy. The big lesson here is that it's smart to check your understanding with someone who knows the language better than you do.

In the end, knowing the real title of the song didn't make the meaning much clearer. I still had a big question: Did the writer of this song, Paul McCartney, mean that he couldn't buy himself love (which made him an even sadder case than Bummy). Or did he just say that no one could buy *his* love?

Great riddles like that—and the lyrics of other songs—made me really learn English. Looking back, I could say that without their lessons, I might never have studied English literature, might never have lived in London and Los Angeles, and might not have become a journalist and a filmmaker. I correspond with English-speaking people every day. (That's another good trick for improving your foreign language skills.)

And by the way, 16 years after I started studying English, I interviewed the writer of "Can Bummy Love?" Before we split, he signed a record for me: "All the best from Paul McCartney—to Ronald."

Hey, Frau Schmidt, if *Ronald* is good enough for a Beatle, it's good enough for me.

Ronald Kruschak is a TV and movie producer for Spiegel Television in Hamburg, Germany. He is also a screenwriter.

HOW TO Learn from Failure

—by John M. Bass

Life is filled with disappointments. For example, in a basketball game, you take a shot, but instead of going through the hoop, the ball bounces off the rim. Engineers label such negative events "failures." When a bridge collapses, we say that it "failed."

Failure can make us feel bad. But here's a surprise. Every failure is a learning opportunity in disguise. By studying a failure, you can often avoid the problem in the future. At the very least, you gain knowledge about how the world works.

To turn failure into learning, engineers use a method called *failure analysis*. Although this system was developed to avoid problems like train wrecks and collapsing dams, it can be applied to many failures that occur in daily life. Here's how to do it.

DIRECTIONS

1. Define exactly what failed. Suppose you get a failing grade on a test. Rather than look at the test as a whole, you need to know exactly which type or types of questions you missed.

2. Find the immediate cause of the failure. Engineers call this cause the "failure mode." Most things can fail in several ways. If you can identify the specific cause, you then know where to focus your energy. For example, in test taking, common failure modes are:

• You didn't read the question correctly.
• You ran out of time or worked too quickly.
• You didn't know how to answer the question.

Each possibility requires a different solution.

continued ...

3. Study the steps that led to the failure.

Often, there is nothing inherently wrong with the thing that failed. The problem could be something leading to the failure. For example, maybe you understood the material on the test but were late to school and had to rush through the questions, which led to making careless errors.

4. Eliminate the cause of the problem so it won't recur. This requires changing how you do things. For example, if you did poorly on the test because you came late, improve your time management skills. On the other hand, if you did not understand the material, you must change your study methods: meet with your teacher for extra help, get a tutor, or spend more time doing practice exercises.

No one is perfect. Each of us makes mistakes every day. All that is needed to be a success is to learn from our mistakes and strive to improve our skills on a daily basis. The key to learning from failure is to ask this simple question: "How can I prevent the problem from happening again?"

John M. Bass is a Registered Professional Engineer, who is licensed in both Electrical and Mechanical Engineering. He specializes in identifying and correcting reliability problems for industrial and aerospace companies. He is the founder and president of Bass Associations, Inc. For more information visit www.BassEngineering.com.

Analyzing a Bicycle Chain Failure

Here's an example of using failure analysis with a common problem. You're riding along on your bike and suddenly the pedals no longer are moving the bike forward. Something is wrong with the chain. There are two likely failure modes:

• *The chain slipped off the sprocket.*
The short-term solution is to put the chain back on. But there is always a reason for a bicycle chain to come off a sprocket. If it was because of a loose chain or poor maintenance, then improve the way you maintain your bike.

• *Your pant leg got caught in the chain.*
You may be tempted to untangle the pant leg and go on your way. But this is the kind of problem that will happen again and again until you study the failure and learn from it. The best way to prevent pants from being caught in the chain is to wear short pants or use a pants clip.

HOW TO Overcome Shyness

—by Art Nefsky

Hi. Remember me? I was the shyest guy in your class. At dances and parties, I used to stand against a wall with my arms folded, trying to look like I was having fun. But I was faking it.

There's nothing wrong with being a little shy. But it's another story if shyness stops you from enjoying life. I've overcome my shyness over the years, and these tips can help you overcome yours.

DIRECTIONS

1. Don't make up excuses to stay home.
Playing computer games or watching "Star Trek" reruns won't help you feel comfortable with people. If you're invited to go to a party, GO! You'll not only get a chance to practice social skills, but you may make new friends.

2. Join a club.
It's always easier spending time with people who share your interests, hobbies, or talents.

3. Perform in public.
This may seem like the last thing you want to do. But nothing helps overcome shyness like getting up in front of people or performing on stage. The turning point in my life was joining the Drama Club. I then went on to become a professional comedian and actor. But you don't have to be a pro. Just performing will help you gain confidence. Try singing, acting, dancing, juggling, debating, telling stories, playing a musical instrument, or whatever you like.

continued ...

4. When having a conversation with someone you don't know very well, show an interest in that person. Ask about the person's hobbies, pets, travels, job, or favorite books. If you're asked a question, give an honest answer, then go right back to talking about the other person. Your conversation partner will think that you're a great person for showing interest.

5. When you have an opinion, express it firmly. Look your listeners in the eye. Not everyone will agree with you, but if you speak from your heart, most people will respect what you have to say.

6. Stop trying to be perfect. For one thing, you can't be. All human beings make mistakes. In fact, many of our most successful performers make mistakes. But they are well liked because they know how to share themselves with others. Trying to hide your flaws will sap your energy. Just be yourself.

7. Never put yourself down. Do you call yourself names in your own head or even in front of others? Stop it! Give yourself a break. If you don't like yourself, how do you expect anyone else to?

8. Make a list of 25 wins. We spend too much time focusing on our disappointments. This can set us up for losing before we get started. To avoid that, fill your mind with thoughts of your victories and accomplishments. Even getting out of bed could be one. To help you focus on what's positive in your life, write that list on paper. Include the little successes as well as the big ones.

9. Be patient. Overcoming shyness is a gradual process and often not so easy. Standing in front of an audience might give you the shakes. But if you practice, you will begin to get used to it and feel good about yourself. And who knows? You may like it so much, you may not want to get out of the spotlight.

Art Nefsky is the founder of Showoffs, a Toronto organization that helps singers, comedians, performers, and others gain confidence. Visit his Web site at www.nefsky.com.

HOW TO Have Good *Manners*
—by Martha Wharton

Manners are rules that help us get along with each other in all sorts of situations. Although we live in fast-changing times, courtesy is always in style. Some of the strategies presented here may seem new or strange to you. But the basic idea is simple: Treat others the way you want to be treated.

DIRECTIONS
1. Greeting People
• *Smile.* Smiling puts the other person at ease.
• *Shake hands.* This is a near-universal sign of friendship. The thumb of your right hand is on top with fingers gripping the other person's right hand. Be firm but don't give a "bone crusher."
• *Tell who you are.* Say, "Hello, my name is _____" and give your name. In many cultures, making eye contact is a key part of the greeting.
• *Introduce others.* When introducing a female and a male, say the female's name first: "Sarah, I'd like to introduce my friend Hank." When introducing people of different ages, say the older person's name first: "Dad, I'd like to introduce my friend Kim." When addressing a woman, young people should include the title *Miss*, *Ms.*, or *Mrs.* Use *Mr.* when talking to a man.

2. Conversing
• Frequently use the words *please, thank you, excuse me,* and *you're welcome.*
• Listen carefully to what the other person says.
• Don't interrupt.
• Ask for the other person's opinion. When someone wants your opinion, respond with more than a one-word answer, but don't talk on and on.
• To end a conversation gracefully, say something like "I've enjoyed talking with you."

Grandpa, I'd like to introduce my friend Julie to you.

continued ...

3. Everyday Table Manners
• Come to the table with your hands washed.
• Don't start eating before others.
• Hold a soup spoon like a pencil. Move it away from you as you lean forward. Sip quietly. When done, leave the spoon in the bowl.
• Cut no more than three pieces of an item at a time. Take small, easy-to-manage bites.
• Keep your mouth closed when chewing.
• Swallow food before taking a drink. Blot your lips to keep the glass rim clean.
• Don't talk with your mouth full. If someone asks you a question, finish chewing, then answer.
• Ask for things. Don't reach across the table.
• Remove small inedible objects from your mouth with your thumb and index finger. Remove larger objects with the fork and place on the plate's edge.
• Pace yourself to finish with everyone else.

4. Formal Dining
• If place cards are used, find your place and stand until others are ready to sit. Don't put your napkin in your lap until the host or hostess does.
• Talk with the people on both sides of you. It is rude to ignore one of your dinner partners.
• Don't slouch. Keep elbows low.
• If you need to leave the table during the meal, put your napkin on your chair. At the end of the meal place the napkin at the left of the plate.
• Drink from the glass to the right of your plate. Use the bread and butter plate on the left.
• If you see several forks and knives, work from the outside in towards the plate for each course. When in doubt, imitate the host or hostess.
• When serving yourself, take medium portions so there will be enough for those who follow you.
• Break off only a small part of bread at a time.

TRICKY-TO-EAT FOODS

• *Finger foods*: After eating French fries, sandwiches, and so on, do not lick your fingers. Wipe them on a napkin.
• *Chicken*: At a picnic, use your fingers; at a restaurant, use a knife and fork.
• *Pizza*: You can eat it with your fingers or with a knife and fork.
• *Spaghetti*: Eat only a few strands at a time. Hint: At a restaurant, if you need to make a good impression, order an easier-to-eat meal.

Martha Wharton is the founder of The Protocol School for Excellence in Palo Alto, California. She presents seminars, workshops, and lectures on etiquette for people of all ages. For more information, visit her Web site: www.protocol-school.com.

HOW TO Remember (Almost) Everything

—by Joel R. Levin

So you want to improve your memory? Exactly how can you do that? Do what? Have you forgotten already? If so, maybe your memory really does need help. Look again at the title of this chapter: *Remember* is the name, and how to remember things better is our aim. So once again, exactly how can you do that? If you do what memory experts do, you'll find out that remembering (almost) everything is as straightforward as 1-2-3. Let me illustrate by applying a systematic method for improving memory—something known as a *mnemonic* (nee-mon-ik) technique.

DIRECTIONS:

1. Undivide your attention. To remember something you must first learn it. Before you learn it, you must give it your full attention. So, begin by focusing on exactly what it is you want to remember. For example, to remember the name of your Aunt Samantha, a person whose name you always forget each time she comes for a visit:

• Concentrate on her facial characteristics.

• Listen carefully when the name is first pronounced.

• Repeat the name aloud or silently after hearing it.

In short, if you don't want it to be "in one ear and out the other," you must care about remembering.

2. Make it meaningful. A new or strange-sounding name is not meaningful. But you can transform the unfamiliar name into a more familiar "word clue" that sounds something like it. For example, you can turn *Samantha* into the word clue *salmon* (the fish). But how will the word clue help you remember Samantha the next time you see her? Good question. Proceed to Step 3 for the answer.

continued ...

3. Create connections. People recall new information best when they build upon previous knowledge—in short, when they make connections between the "old" and the "new." If ready-made connections are not available, create your own. In the case of remembering a person's name:

• Find something "special" about the person whose name you want to remember. Suppose, for example, that when you look at Aunt Samantha, the first thing you notice is her teeth. They might be perfectly spaced, glistening white, large, or lined with gold fillings. Whatever the reason, if you notice her teeth, they become your partner in remembering.

• Make up a little story or scene that involves the word clue (Step 2) and that detail about the person (in our example, Samantha's teeth). For example, imagine that a salmon with giant glistening teeth is about to bite into a fishing hook, or that a salmon is grinning at you as you walk past the fish section of the supermarket. Adding action to the scene or exaggerating the size of the teeth will help you remember better. If you concentrate on seeing the toothy salmon picture in your mind, the next time you meet Aunt Samantha, her teeth will remind you of the scene with the salmon, which in turn will zero you in on the target, your aunt's name.

Now you have the three principles for remembering. Oops, I almost "forgot" (certainly not a word that belongs in this lesson). There's a fourth ingredient. It's a universal principle that can be applied to the skills referred to in (almost) every chapter in this book, whether it's becoming skilled at playing a musical instrument or training your dog to catch a Frisbee. The fourth principle is:

4. Practice. If you frequently remind yourself that the name of your "aunt with the teeth" is Samantha, the next time you meet her, you'll more likely say, "Hello, Auntie Samantha" than "Hello, Auntie Fish!"

MEMORY-IMPROVEMENT TECHNIQUES IN ACTION

You can use memory-improvement techniques to remember word meanings, lists of ordered items, and even facts that are taught in school. Here's an example.

WHAT'S A DAHLIA?

To remember that a dahlia is a flower, simply apply the four steps from the lesson:

1. Undivide your attention. Focus on the word *dahlia* and its meaning (flower).
2. Make *dahlia* meaningful by transforming it into the word clue *doll*.
3. Create a connection between a doll and a flower by clearly picturing a child's doll sniffing a beautiful flower.
4. Practice by asking yourself: "What is a dahlia? Dahlia reminds me of doll, and doll reminds me of the scene where a doll is sniffing a flower. Therefore, a dahlia is a flower."

The more you work at it, the more (memory) power to you!

Joel R. Levin is a Distinguished Professor of Educational Psychology at the University of Wisconsin— Madison. For the past 30 years, he has been conducting research on techniques for improving memory, with more than 200 published articles and books on that topic. He claims to be able to remember (almost) every one of those publications!

HOW TO Be Adventurous

—by Erling Kagge

One of my good friends, Arne Naess, is a mountain climber. When someone asked him why he kept on climbing, Arne replied, "Why did you quit?"

I have lived a very privileged life. I skied to the North Pole with Borge Ousland as the first unsupported expedition there. I walked to the South Pole in 50 days in total solitude, the first person to do so. And later, I climbed Mount Everest. It is not my place to recommend that you do what I have done. But I do recommend that every person find a challenge and try to achieve it.

DIRECTIONS

1. Dream with abandon. Don't limit yourself just because something seems out of the ordinary or unreachable.

2. Choose your future goals based on your dreams. The goals should be specific, something you can imagine accomplishing.

3. Think how in the world you can reach each goal. Figure out what training you will need and how you will get it.

4. Keep dreaming. Although I am getting older, I keep on being curious like a child. I do believe that curiosity is the only trait that people who reach beyond themselves have in common. Because, if you can dream it, you can do it.

The trail to reaching your dream may not be easy, but no one ever achieved a dream by sleeping too long.

Erling Kagge is one of the world's most renowned explorers. He is also a lawyer and the author of *Pole to Pole & Beyond*, a book about some of his adventures.

129

HOW TO Be Creative

—by Roger von Oech

Over the past 20 years, I've worked with creative people in many fields. Again and again, I've noticed a pattern. Creative people have mental flexibility. Like race-car drivers who shift gears as they move around the course, creative people shift in and out of different types of thinking. Depending on the needs of the situation, they'll be open, playful, critical, or persistent.

From this I've learned that creativity consists of four roles: Explorer, Artist, Judge, Warrior. Each focuses on a thinking style that you can practice.

DIRECTIONS

1. Be an Explorer. As a creative thinker, you need the raw materials from which new ideas are made, including facts, experiences, knowledge, and feelings. You are much more likely to find something original if you venture off the beaten path. Try some of the following strategies:
- Ask "why?"
- Dig deeper.
- Change viewpoints.
- See! Hear! Taste! Feel! Smell!
- Listen to your dreams.
- Look to nature.

2. Be an Artist. The materials you gather will be like pieces of colored glass in a kaleidoscope. They may form a pattern, but if you want something new, you'll have to give them a twist. Let the Artist in you come out. Experiment. Follow your intuition. You can rearrange things, look at them backwards, and turn them upside down. Other Artist strategies you might try are:
- Ask "What If" questions.
- Simplify.
- Exaggerate.
- Rearrange or combine ideas.

continued ...

3. Be a Judge. Now ask yourself, "Is this idea any good? Is it worth pursuing? Do I have the resources to make it happen?" Critically weigh the evidence. Ask someone to attack your idea so that you can discover its weaknesses. Other Judge strategies are:

- Solve the right problem.
- Focus on what's important.
- Be dissatisfied.
- Don't be a know-it-all.
- Listen to your hunches.

4. Be a Warrior. The world isn't ready for every new idea that comes along. If you want your idea to succeed, you must take it into battle. As a Warrior, you are part general and part foot soldier. You need courage to overcome excuses, setbacks, and other obstacles. Warrior strategies that can help you turn your idea into reality are:

- Believe in yourself.
- Get support.
- Don't bother with excuses.
- Do the unexpected.
- Set a deadline.
- Be persistent.
- Learn from mistakes.

Sometimes you'll go through all four roles in a short period. Suppose you're working on a project and someone asks a difficult question. Your Explorer will comb through your mind looking for facts that answer the question. Your Artist will mold these into an answer. Your Judge will decide if the answer is appropriate. And your Warrior will confidently deliver the response.

Sometimes you may spend a long time in each of the roles. Suppose you're putting on a variety show to raise money for a good cause. You may spend days as an Explorer doing research to find talent. You may spend an equal time as an Artist and a Judge developing and refining the show. And finally, you may spend weeks as a Warrior publicizing the program and handling all the details.

STRENGTHENING YOUR CREATIVE ROLES

I have a friend who's a competent Explorer, an outstanding Artist, an OK Judge, and a lousy Warrior. As a result, he comes up with wonderful ideas that never go anywhere. Another friend is mediocre in the first three roles, but a ferocious Warrior. As a result, she brings to reality many moderately innovative ideas. A third friend has a strong Artist and Explorer, a weak Judge, and a tremendous Warrior. As you might expect, he puts terrific and terrible ideas into action. What do we learn from these people?

• *Develop all four roles.* Ask yourself: How adventurous is my Explorer? How imaginative is my Artist? How reliable is my Judge? How persistent is my Warrior?

• *Know when it makes sense to shift from one role to another.* As with most things in life, timing is essential. Wearing a bathing suit to the beach makes sense. Wearing a bathing suit to meet the President makes the Secret Service uneasy. Similarly, adopting a role at the wrong time can be counter-productive.

Be creative—enjoy the theater of your mind!

Roger von Oech is a well-known creativity consultant. He's the author of the best-selling book *A Whack on the Side of the Head* and a companion set of cards entitled *Creative Whack Pack*.

PART 6

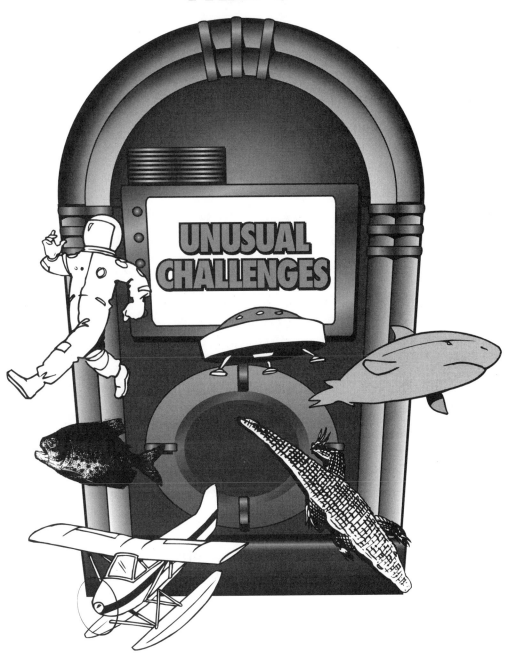

UNUSUAL
CHALLENGES

HOW TO Be a Private Eye

—by Charles T. Rahn

I'm a private investigator, also known as a "private detective" or "private eye." The job is not like what you see on TV or in the movies. I don't get involved in high-speed chases or acrobatic fights. But I find the work fascinating and challenging. If you want to try it yourself, here are the facts.

DIRECTIONS

1. Become known in your community.
Running a private investigation business is like running any business: you need customers ("clients"). I advertise in the phone book and on the Internet. I also join community groups so that people get to know me. I make a big effort to meet attorneys because many of their cases require finding facts, and fact-finding is my specialty.

2. Figure out what the client wants. When
potential clients enter your office, they can be upset and confused about what they expect you to do. Before you agree to take a case, interview the person to learn the details of the job.

3. Know how to find information. Start
by asking questions. In the old days, P.I. work was done by walking around town and talking to people. All that walking frequently led to getting gum on their shoes, and this is where the term "gumshoe" came from. Modern P.I.s rely more and more on the Internet! You can practice this skill if you have an online computer. Use a search engine to find public information about yourself or about someone in the news.

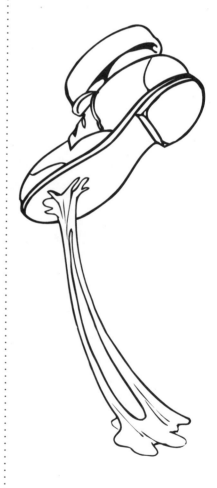

continued ...

4. Develop your camera skills. Photography and videography are important, especially for documenting accident and crime scenes. But you need to know how to properly capture a scene so that the pictures will be useful as evidence. Take a photography course, and spend time in court watching how visuals are used.

5. Be careful. There is always an element of danger in P.I. work because you're dealing with the unknown. You may come across people who don't want the truth to come out. Common sense is a good guide. You must be prepared for any situation that may arise.

6. Write your report. Include the key evidence you collected plus a description of the facts. And remember, "Just the facts, please." Then be prepared for the client to react emotionally. The truth can hurt, and some people can't handle it even though they hired you to be their eyes and ears.

7. Don't give up if you're not always successful. As in all of life, things may not come out the way you wanted. Some cases are easier to solve than others. My success rate in helping clients find people, including long-lost relatives or friends, is about 95%. On the other hand, it's rare that I can help someone accused of a crime get off because most law enforcement agencies build strong cases.

In my experience, the most successful P.I.s have law enforcement training. Police officers are inquisitive by their nature. However, some good P.I.s come from other fields. Whatever your background, to be a good P.I. requires intelligence, patience, common sense, and a desire to help people. You'll get many rewards if you do the job well. Every day presents new challenges because no two cases are identical. And making one person happy can outweigh all the sad, boring times.

Charles T. Rahn is the founder of A Very Private Eye, Inc., in Orlando, Florida. His Web site is: orlandoonline.com/pi.htm. You can e-mail him at: averyprivateeye@Juno.com.

HOW TO Outsmart Piranhas
—by Walter Glaser

Piranhas can be very nasty fish. But they are not all that way. Not even the bad ones are always terrible. But when they are, there is only one rule: STAY OUT OF THEIR WAY!

Piranhas live in South America—in parts of the Amazon and in nearby rivers of the tropical rain forest basin. They are disc-shaped, and range in color from olive-green to blue-black to silver, with an underlying tinge of orange or red on their bellies.

These fish have sharp teeth—very sharp indeed. So sharp, and with such an edge, that you can't catch them with ordinary nylon fishing line. To fish them successfully, you have to use a stainless-steel wire lead that they can't easily bite through.

But are all piranhas dangerous? Well, no, they're not. Surprisingly, most of these species are vegetarian. They live on the fruits and nuts that fall into the rivers and leave swimmers alone.

However, a small number of varieties are meaner. Like their vegetarian cousins, these piranhas grow to around 18 inches (50 cm), have similar coloring, and eat fruits and nuts when available. But they have sharper teeth, and when they cannot get fruits and nuts, they eat fish and meat.

In the rainy season, the river levels are high and there is more food, so piranhas mostly leave people alone. But in the dry season, the waters of the Amazon recede, often stranding schools of piranha in places where they cannot find enough food. Then the carnivorous ones attack and try to eat anything. They bite chunks out of each other's fins. If they had a chance, they would bite chunks out of you. Here are some rules to make sure that doesn't happen.

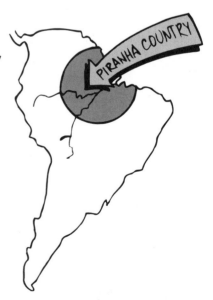

DIRECTIONS

1. Never go into the water to swim without checking it out. Always ask locals if it is safe.

2. Never go into the water if you have cuts or bruises. Piranhas can smell the blood and it makes them very hungry and dangerous.

3. Watch where the Amazon Indians and other locals swim. Piranhas don't like water that is too acidic or alkaline. They stay out of such water and prefer the river parts that are more comfortable for them. Some tributaries of the Amazon are like that—too acid or too alkaline. The local people know which are the places to swim and feel safe. So ask where these safe rivers are, and only swim there.

4. Be careful when fishing for piranhas. You can catch piranhas with a hand line from a boat or a pier, but be very careful that you keep your hands away from their mouths. Even after you catch them, they can give you a nasty bite.

PIRANHAS FOR DINNER

Now you know how not to get eaten by piranhas, but can you eat them? The answer is yes, you can eat piranhas. They taste like snapper. Delicious. And how do you cook them? Clean and scale them like any other fish, cut diagonal scores on the skin, and grill or fry as soon after catching as possible.

If you can't catch your own piranha, don't worry. Every fish market along the Amazon and nearby rivers usually sells lots of piranha varieties, both the vegetarian and carnivorous ones.

And it's much better for you if you eat them than the other way around.

Walter Glaser is a professional writer who lives in Melbourne, Australia. His articles on food, travel, humor, business, and adventure have appeared in *The Los Angeles Times*, *The Financial Times* (London), *The Manchester Guardian*, *Far East Traveler*, and *Fodor's Guide to Australia*.

HOW TO Get Out of Quicksand
—by R. Ted Jeo

Quicksand is found near some beaches, marshes, and streams. It forms when sand collects in hollows and becomes totally saturated with water. This happens if clay lining the hollow keeps the water from draining. Sometimes, mud and vegetation mix with the wet sand. This thick form of quicksand looks solid, and even feels solid if touched lightly. But if you step on it, the material immediately liquifies and you'll sink.

Quicksand can be scary, but if you know how to react, you can escape.

DIRECTIONS

1. Avoid trouble in the first place. If you are visiting an area that might contain quicksand, ask local authorities for advice. If in doubt, carry a long pole to probe the ground ahead for possible problem spots.

2. If you find yourself sinking into quicksand, don't panic. Quicksand will not "suck" you down. Because your body is less dense than the density of the thick sand-water mixture, your whole body will not sink below the surface.

3. Don't struggle. Thrashing around interferes with your natural flotation and will make you sink faster. It will also tire you out. If you relax, you will just float on the surface.

4. Look for something to grab. Try to reach for grasses or roots, or for overhanging branches.

continued ...

QUICKSAND ETYMOLOGY

Quick in *quicksand* doesn't mean "fast." It comes from an ancient word meaning "alive." Perhaps people used that word because the wet sand seemed almost to be a living thing. *Quick* has the same meaning in *quicksilver*.

QUICKSAND RESCUE EFFORT

If someone else falls into quicksand, do not go into the quicksand yourself to pull the person out! You must remain on solid ground in order to help. Do the following:

• Keep the person calm by talking in a relaxed voice.

• Remind the person to float on his or her back.

• If you have a rope, tie one end to a strong anchoring item, such as a tree, and throw the other end to the person. If you don't have a rope, use branches, roots, your belt, or any other sturdy article of clothing.

• If the rope or rope substitute is not long enough, or if there is nothing firm to anchor it to, lie on your stomach and reach toward the person. But make sure you stay out of the quicksand, and be careful that the other person does not pull you in.

5. If you start sinking because of your efforts to escape, stop moving. Catch your breath and become calm. Drop any type of heavy items that you might be carrying, for example, a backpack.

6. Turn slowly onto your back with your arms stretched. Float as if you were in a swimming pool. Floating on your back is the best position to keep your head above the surface.

7. Move your body slowly toward the nearest firm ground. Do this by making slow rocking motions and gently paddling with your hands. Try not to disturb the quicksand. If you feel yourself sinking, stop and allow the quicksand to thicken. Be patient. It might take some time, but eventually you will work your way to firm ground.

R. Ted Jeo is a physical geographer. In addition to his professional work, he is one of a group of scientists who answer questions sent to the Mad Scientist Network (http://madsci.wustl.edu).

HOW TO Live on a  Submarine
—by Ron Martini

Life on a submarine can be as fascinating as space travel. In fact, planners of space missions study the experiences of submariners. If you'd like to live and work underwater, let me give you a few pointers based on the many voyages I took aboard nuclear subs. As we say in the navy, "All ahead full!"

DIRECTIONS

1. Know how a submarine sinks and rises. Like all boats, subs float because they weigh less than the water they push aside. But unlike ordinary boats, submarines can change their weight. To dive, you and your shipmates open valves that let water flow into tanks. To bring the boat to the surface, you pump water out of the tanks.

2. Be able to live without seeing the sun. Military subs can stay below the surface for about two months. There are no windows on these boats. But even if there were, you wouldn't see anything. Sunlight reaches only to a depth of about 50 feet (17 meters). Subs travel deeper than that, so most of the time they move through pitch-black water.

3. Get along with people. If you can't keep your emotions under control, don't think about becoming a submariner. Crew members must work together in close quarters to carry out their mission. The boat's doctor is trained to deal with any activity that may upset the delicate balance of harmony and friendship.

4. Follow orders. On a military sub, there are levels of command. Crew members at each level must follow the orders given them by their officers.

5. Be flexible. On a submarine, each crew member usually does more than one job. For example, besides treating those who get sick, the medical staff also monitors the quality of the air.

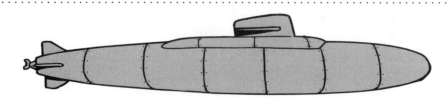

QUESTIONS & ANSWERS ABOUT SUBMARINES

How big is a submarine? A military sub is as long as two football fields (200 meters) and as tall as a four-story building. It carries from 90 to 125 sailors.

How does the crew "see" underwater? A device called sonar emits sounds that bounce off other ships or undersea mountains. The echo warns the crew that something is ahead. Bats use a similar system known as echolocation.

How is food prepared? There are three cooks aboard. Sailors eat in groups of 25 in a dining room called the "Crews' mess."

How do you breathe underwater? The air on a sub is purer than air on the surface. Oxygen is made from sea water by electrolysis. Offensive gasses and odors are eliminated by filters, chemicals, and burning.

What happens if you get sick or injured? The medical staff consists of a doctor and an assistant. If an operation is needed, the officers' wardroom table becomes an operating table. If necessary, the ship will surface and radio for help.

What are routine activities? The crew is divided into three groups, or "watches." Sailors are on duty for six hours and off for twelve. Classes are held regularly so that sailors can gain additional skills. Recreational activities include: watching movies, reading, playing games such as chess and backgammon, and exercising. A floating wire strung out behind the ship connects to a floating antenna and brings radio news and family messages. Church services are held each Sunday, and discussion groups meet throughout the week.

Ron Martini served on the USS Catfish SS339 and the USS Patrick Henry SSBN 599. Visit his Web site: wavecom.net/~rontini.

HOW TO Handle an Airplane *Emergency!*
—by David Littlefield

Imagine that you're a passenger in a small plane. Suddenly, the pilot loses consciousness. You are the only one who can get the airplane back to the airport. But you don't know how to fly an airplane, much less land it. There are dozens of switches, knobs, dials, gauges, and controls, and you have no idea what they do.

Not long ago, Leland Capps found himself in this situation. My job, as an air traffic controller, was to help Leland deal with this crisis. Thanks largely to his ability to stay calm, he was able to do it. The transcript, starting on page 144, shows exactly what happened.

If you follow a few simple steps, you might be able to work your way out of a similar predicament.

DIRECTIONS

Step 1. Before taking off, ask the pilot to show you how to use the radio. If there is a problem, you will be able to call for help.

Step 2. Know what kind of plane you're in. This will allow the people on the ground to visualize the controls and know how to guide you.

Step 3. As the pilot flies the plane, ask about the controls and instruments. You won't be able to learn everything, but you might pick up a few basics that could come in handy. (See the diagram on the next page. It's a simplified drawing of the basic controls.)

continued ...

Step 4. Be aware of landmarks that you're flying over. These might include large buildings, rivers or lakes, or other noticeable features. As you'll see when you read the transcript, Leland was able to let the people on the ground know where he was by naming a landmark that he could see from the air.

Step 5. If an emergency happens, tell yourself to keep calm. Panic can be deadly. You need to keep your wits about you as you begin to work on a very difficult problem—how to fly and land a plane. Don't make any rash moves. In many cases, a plane will probably stay level until you change a setting.

Step 6. Use the radio to ask for help. You will have to press a microphone button to communicate with air traffic control. Begin by saying that you have an emergency.

Step 7. Release the button and listen carefully to whatever the air traffic controller says. Follow the instructions as well as you can. If you are unsure at any point, ask questions until you understand what you have been told. In the story, beginning on the next page, a pilot suffered a heart attack and could no longer fly the plane. But the passenger-turned-pilot remained calm, followed my instructions, and walked away from the damaged aircraft without a scratch.

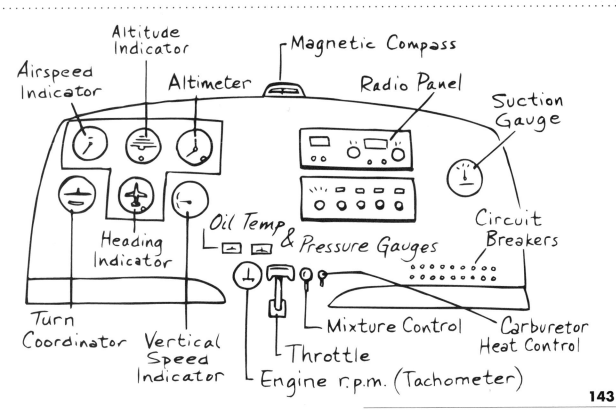

TROUBLE IN THE SKY

At 2:09 p.m. on March 20, 1996, a small seaplane took off from Lake Washington outside Seattle. On board were the pilot, Raymond Ihrke, and his passenger, Leland Capps. That afternoon, I was working as supervisor in the nearby Renton Airport Control Tower. At 2:25, a message came in over the loudspeaker. At that moment, controller David Shettleroe was handling flights.

In this transcript, "N60M" is the registration number (call sign) of the airplane. "Renton" is used for messages from the control tower. Words in brackets give background information.

N60M: I'm in trouble up here. My pilot's passed out on me. I need somebody there to take care of him when I get in if I ever do.

Renton: OK, I'm with you, sir. Can you tell me where you are?

N60M: Somewhere close to Microsoft.

[*Microsoft is a computer company in Redmond, Washington, east of Lake Washington. Clearly, the passenger had been observing landmarks.*]

Renton: OK, do you have control of the aircraft, sir?

N60M: As best I can, yes, sir.

Renton: Are you a pilot?

N60M: No, sir, I'm not.

Renton: OK, I'm going to put a pilot on with you. We're going to get you back to the airport.

[*David Shettleroe gave me the mike. The pilot he had in mind was me! From here on, the words after* **Renton** *are what I said to the man in the plane.*]

Renton: Sir, do you have the wings level? What's your name, sir?

[*There was no response. In pilot training, the key lesson is "Always fly the airplane first." The passenger-turned-pilot might be trying to control the airplane, so I gave him a little time to answer. Then I tried again.*]

Renton: Airplane in distress over Microsoft, are you there? Can you hear me? Are you able to call me on the radio?

continued …

N60M:　　Yes, I forgot to press the button. I'm sorry.

[*To send messages on an aircraft radio, you need to push the microphone button to transmit.*]

Renton:　　Are the wings level on the airplane?

N60M:　　Yes, they are level.

Renton:　　OK, I want you to turn towards Renton now, but very gently. If you turn the control wheel to the left, the airplane will turn to the left. It's like a bicycle. If the wings are not level, the airplane will turn, so I want you to get the airplane banked about ten degrees and then turn towards Renton. Tell me if you're able to do that.

N60M:　　OK, I'm doing it. I can see Seattle now real well.

Renton:　　Can you tell me what kind of airplane you're in?

N60M:　　A 185.

[*This was good news. A 185 is a Cessna. I had flown many Cessna-built planes though not 185s.*]

Renton:　　Does it have a tail wheel?

N60M:　　We're on floats, sir.

[*This was NOT good news. I'm not licensed to fly a seaplane. But a Cessna is a Cessna. You pull back on the yoke to go up, push in to go down. Even though it has floats and not wheels, it responds the same as other airplanes while in the air. However, landing on water is different than landing on land!*]

Renton:　　On floats, OK. Is the pilot totally incapacitated?

N60M:　　Yes, sir.

[*My coworkers were calling the airport rescue team and arranging for radar to track the plane.*]

Renton:　　OK, make sure that he remains off the controls. Try and restrain him with his shoulder strap.

N60M:　　He's passed out completely. He was coughing up blood.

Renton:　　We have an ambulance here. What is your first name, sir?

continued …

N60M: Leland.

Renton: All right, Leland, my name's Dave. How high up are you?

N60M: The altimeter says almost seven.

[*This meant that the plane was 700 feet (200 meters) above the ground.*]

Renton: Do you have me in sight yet?

N60M: Yes, I do. We're going across the Mercer Island Bridge.

[*This bridge is five miles—eight kilometers—from the airport.*]

Renton: I have you in sight. Leland, I need you to find the manifold pressure gauge. It's going to say something between 0 and 30 inches.

[*This gauge indicates the power output from the engine.*]

N60M: I see it.

Renton: Pull the throttle back a little. See if the pointer goes down.

[*The throttle controls the engine's power output. If you pull on the throttle knob, the engine and propeller slow.*]

N60M: It's between 15 and 20.

Renton: Tell me your airspeed. It's in the left-hand side of the panel.

N60M: About 115.

[*Airplane speed is measured in "knots." A speed of 115 knots equals about 130 miles per hour (210 kilometers per hour).*]

Renton: That's very good. Now, I need you to find a little handle that's on the panel. It's labeled flaps.

[*This control lowers a section on the wing so that the plane can fly at a slower speed. This adjustment is used for take-offs and landings. About 15 switches are located near the flap control, but Leland didn't panic.*]

N60M: I found it.

Renton: OK. Hold that down for about six seconds, then put it back to neutral. That made you climb higher, didn't it?

N60M: Yes it did.

[*Leland now was too high to land on this approach. He would have to fly over the airport, circle back, and make another approach.*]

continued ...

Renton: Do you want to try and set it down on the water or do you want to try and set it down on the grass?

N60M: Which would be the safest?

Renton: If you put it on the grass, you might have a good chance.

N60M: I want to make sure that I get him to a hospital.

Renton: OK. Now I want you to push that flap button down.

[*As a plane slows for a landing, the pilot needs to add more flaps.*]

N60M: How's that look?

Renton: Good. Now pull the power back to about 12. You're doing a really good job. OK, start a left turn now. Line up on the grass area. Cinch your seat belt down real tight. Put one hand on the controls and one hand on the throttle.

N60M: OK.

Renton: As soon as you cross the shoreline, I want you to slowly pull the power off, and then slowly pull the control wheel back.

[*During a landing approach the nose should point slightly up. Leland followed my directions. Unfortunately, the plane descended too quickly and splashed into the lake, about 400 feet (120 meters) short of the shoreline. It bounced 200 feet (60 meters) into the air. Because the nose was pointed too high and the power was almost off, the plane was quickly losing airspeed. In seconds, all control would be lost.*]

Renton: Add power, Leland! Lower the nose! Add power!

[*Leland followed my instructions, but now the plane was diving too fast.*]

Renton: Power off! Power off!

[*Leland saw the view out the window and knew he was about to crash. He pulled back on the wheel, which brought the plane to level flight just before the floats struck the ground, followed by the right wing. The plane skidded off the runway, went through the grassy area, and stopped.*]

Renton: Pull the power off. Can you hear me? Are you there?

N60M: Yes, I'm here. Sorry about the landing.

David Littlefield has been an air traffic controller for 15 years. He also holds a commercial pilot license and is a certified flight instructor.

HOW TO Help Your Pet Become a ★ Star

—by Kay Cox

Have you ever dreamed that your pet would appear on TV or in the movies? It takes lots of work and patience, plus having the right pet for the job. A bit of luck helps, too.

Some pets love to show off. They naturally enjoy the stage, the spotlight, and all the attention. Other animals are more private and prefer to stay in the background.

If your pet is a "performer," then you might want to begin developing tricks that will dazzle your friends and may lead to a career in show business. Do you have time each day to coach your pet? If yes, let's get started.

DIRECTIONS

1. Begin with the basics. The first actions to teach your pet are *Sit*, *Come*, *Down*, *Stay*, and *Heel*. Practice these tricks in a positive way so that your pet will enjoy doing them for you. Give lots of love and treats for good performances. Cats and birds can be taught to do tricks as well as dogs, but you may need a little more patience.

2. Build on natural behaviors. Watch to see what tricks your pet does naturally. Some pets are great jumpers; have them jump through a hoop. Some sit up to beg for treats; teach them to sit up on command. Some use a paw as a hand; teach them to shake hands. Pets that like to carry things can be trained to tote a basket. Dogs can be taught to bark when asked. Cats can be trained to climb a ladder. Bunnies can learn to put a letter in a mailbox.

continued ...

GET AN AGENT

A pet agent is important for many reasons. A good agent will:

• Arrange for publicity and for opportunities to get your pet seen by TV and movie producers.

• Advise you on the nuts and bolts of an audition—what materials to bring, how long the tryout will last, where to stand, when to be silent, and other procedures.

• Negotiate a contract that will fairly pay you for your pet's talent. Be aware that many things can happen on a TV or movie set that could put you in legal trouble if you don't have a contract.

3. Practice the tricks in many settings. Your pet must enjoy doing his tricks whenever asked, performing them at a distance from you, and repeating them over and over. The act may have to be done in places that are crowded, noisy, bright, and hot. Many pets have no problem doing tricks at home, but are nervous in unfamiliar places. If they react by snapping or scratching when startled by strangers or unusual sounds, they won't get the job. A successful pet performer must be friendly to all, including small children and other animals.

4. Be patient. Show your pet lots of love. Be generous with treats. Train your pet one trick at a time and be sure he knows that trick very well before you start on another.

GENERAL TRAINING TIPS

• Enjoy what you are doing. Pets respond to a positive attitude, and you'll have more fun, too.

• Never become so tied to an idea that you cannot change and grow. If your pet can't master one trick, try something new.

• Always do the very best you can do and expect excellence from your pet.

• Realize how important your support group is. Family and friends are sounding boards that help you keep on target.

• Remember that "giving" in a relationship is more important than "getting." This includes giving to a pet.

DOG TRICKS

Teaching tricks is easier if the dog has been obedience trained, but it can be done without formal training. Each trick should have separate and distinct commands or signals NOT associated with obedience commands. This way your dog won't get confused about what you want him to do. Teach one trick at a time. Don't start on a second trick until your dog knows the first one!

If your dog shows a natural tendency toward a trick, encourage it! For instance, a dog who jumps a lot can be taught to jump rope easier than a non-jumping dog. A dog who uses his nose to nudge things can easily be taught to push a ball or turn on a switch with his nose.

Enjoy teaching some of these tricks, and make up your own as you go along.

Take a Bow: When your dog stretches, he puts his front feet out, his head down, and his tail up in the air. Watch him and when he does this, always say, "Take a bow." Praise him and give him a reward. After a few times he will "bow" on command.

Walk on Hind Legs: If your dog stands on his hind legs naturally, this trick is easy to teach. Hold food over his head and slowly walk backwards. Command "Walk" and "Good boy." Reward and praise. After he understands the command, train him to walk from one person to another or to where you have placed his reward. When asking him to "Walk," always hold the reward up high.

Dance: After teaching "Walk," hold the food directly overhead and circle it so your dog walks in a circle. Use the command "Dance" for this trick. If you add music, your dog will try to keep time as you move the reward fast or slow. Costumes, such as a hat and ruffle, make this trick special.

continued ...

Push a Cart: Set a brick in front of a doll carriage so it won't move. Train your dog to put his paws on the handle to get a reward. When he is comfortable with this, remove the brick and stand in front of the carriage. Slowly back up and give the "Walk" command. Hold the reward up and slowly back away. DO NOT RUSH THIS TRICK. A dog may need several days to catch on. You may even need to hold his paws on the handle and walk with him at first. Work on this trick for a few minutes a day.

Retrieve: A neat trick is to have the dog bring back specific objects on command.

Begin by teaching the names of three objects, such as a ball, a fake dumbbell labeled 1000 pounds (450 kilograms), and keys. First throw the ball and say, "Go get the ball." Next, put the ball in the yard and tell your dog to "Go get the ball." Then remove the ball and in the same way teach the dog to fetch the dumbbell and the keys.

Now place the ball and the dumbbell side by side. Tell your dog to "Go get the ball." Give a reward only when he brings the ball. Repeat this activity for a day or two. Then place the dumbbell and keys in the yard but NOT the ball.

Now ask your dog to "Go get the dumbbell." Only reward when he brings the dumbbell. After a day or two you can put the dumbbell and the ball in the yard. Ask your dog to "Go get the ball" a few times. Only reward for bringing the ball. Then change and ask for the dumbbell. With patience, you can get your dog to bring only the item you ask for. Don't forget to hug and reward with a treat for each time he brings the right item.

Remember: Be patient and work on one trick at a time until your dog knows it well. Then start a new one. End each session with a review of the tricks he already knows. This should be a fun time. Never work longer than a half hour at a time on tricks.

Kay Cox is an animal psychologist and talent agent. She specializes in behavior modification and inter-species communication. She hosts "The Pet Corner," a radio show in Arizona. For more information, visit her Web site: www.getnet.com/~petcouns.

HOW TO Hike Safely in Bear Country
—by the North Cascades National Park Staff

Because bears are individuals, there are no precise rules about what to do if you encounter one. Every instance is different. What works best cannot be predicted with certainty. However, there are generally effective measures to be followed.

DIRECTIONS

1. Keep a clean camp. Use animal-resistant food boxes. If the campground lacks a secure food storage box, hang your food bag in a tree at least 100 yards (90 meters) from your tent. It should be on a branch 10 feet (3 meters) above the ground, and positioned 4 feet (1.2 meters) from the trunk.

2. Stay alert to your surroundings. Be extra wary in places with food favored by bears, such as berries or carcasses of large animals. If you smell a dead animal, do not investigate! Leave the area and inform a ranger.

3. Don't startle a bear. If you can't see far ahead, or if flowing water muffles sounds, make noise as you hike. Talk, sing, shout, or clap your hands. Avoid high-pitched noises as these may attract bears. Some hikers use bells, but these may arouse a bear's curiosity.

4. Be cautious when hiking at dawn or dusk. Bears can be active throughout the day or night, but they are most often met early or late in the day.

5. If possible, do not hike alone. Bears are less likely to approach a group. When hiking with small children, be sure they always stay with you.

6. Keep dogs leashed and under your control. Loose dogs disturb wildlife and may lead a bear back to you.

continued ...

7. Be watchful when walking off trail. Bears may rest or sleep next to a log, in dense brush, or in a grassy meadow.

8. Don't approach a bear to photograph it or for any other reason. If it hasn't seen you, calmly exit the area while talking aloud so it knows you are moving away. Most bears will leave when they see or hear you.

9. If you can't avoid a bear, shake leafy branches or snap limbs. Bears snap branches to tell each other not to come too close. As you make these noises, keep talking in a loud, low tone.

10. Do not come between a bear and her cubs. Bears are very protective of their offspring.

11. If a bear moves toward you, don't scream, run, or make sudden moves. You can't outrun a bear, and screaming may upset it. Don't shoot the bear because a wound may anger it.

12. If a bear wants to "check you out," avoid eye contact. The bear may stand up to identify what you are, not to threaten you. If you hold still, the bear may leave. Bears rarely attack unless threatened. Talking in low, soothing tones may help keep you calm. Do not panic.

North Cascades National Park is located in the Cascades, a mountain range that extends from Washington State in the U.S. to British Columbia in Canada.

13. If a bear approaches quickly, drop a hat or other object. Move away without running. The bear may stop to examine what you have dropped.

14. If a black bear attacks, fight back. Use rocks, sticks, equipment, or your hands if nothing else is available. Aim for the bear's eyes or nose.

15. If a grizzly bear attacks and you can't flee, drop into a "cannonball position." Keep your neck and face between your knees. If the bear takes you out of this position, try to resume it. Usually the bear will see that you are not a threat and will leave you alone. Don't take the offensive against a bear with cubs.

16. Use a bear repellent only as a last resource. Even effective repellents, such as pepper spray, work only at close range. Depending on them could endanger you.

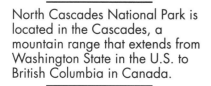

HOW TO Invent Things

—by Larry Shultz

When I was a kid, I heard about inventors making lots of money while helping the world and becoming famous. I always hoped that I would be lucky enough to invent something equally valuable. But I learned that invention isn't mainly about luck. It takes time and energy. You must push, push, and push to make it happen.

Here are a few hints that may help you become a successful inventor.

DIRECTIONS

1. Read about inventors. As a kid I read about Thomas Edison, Alexander Graham Bell, Leonardo da Vinci, and other geniuses. But for me, the ultimate inventor is Nikola Tesla. Everyone should read about him. He's not as famous as many lesser inventors, and he died penniless. Yet he changed the world.

2. Pay attention to your ideas. You can't sit down and say, "Today I'll invent X." You live your life and filter a lot of ideas. These might come from reading or talking to people. If something is relevant, it rises to the top of your consciousness and cries out for attention.

For me, the process usually starts with a problem. For example, after I bought a car that didn't have an air bag for the front passenger seat, I wanted to install one. Then I realized if I could solve that problem, the invention would be useful to millions of people who owned older cars.

3. Keep track of your ideas. Always have a paper and pencil or pen available. I also carry a pocket tape recorder. You never know when a good idea or inspiration will arise. And when it does, you don't want to forget it.

It won't fit me!

continued ...

4. Be critical. Sometimes what you think is a good idea may not be worth all the time, money, and trouble to get that idea developed. If you present the same idea to family members, friends, or business people and the vast majority think it is not a good idea, listen to them. They all may be wrong, but maybe they see something you don't. It takes many other people to help you on the road to manufacturing and selling a product. Usually, you'll get further if you focus your energy on an idea that many people agree is a great idea.

5. Build a team. Few people have all the skills needed to turn an idea into a finished product. I usually work with an engineer or a group of people who do the technical duties.

6. Have faith. The hardest part of being an inventor is not knowing if you are spending hours and days and sometimes years on a product that might not become successful.

7. Be flexible. Don't quickly give up, even when all hope seems lost. Change your angle of attack, go to sleep and "dream" on it, do whatever you can to keep your idea alive. Focus on it in an entirely new way in order to break through a problem you may be having.

8. Enjoy what you're doing. You won't be good at your job if you don't enjoy it.

Larry Shultz has invented many things. These include TickeTV (a scrambling system used by pay-per-view TV systems), the Interactor (which allows video game players to "feel" sound), and the IntelliFlow Care Bag (an advanced automobile passenger safety system). He also develops ideas and stories for books, TV, and motion pictures.

THE INTERACTOR

• **Idea.** At a demonstration for a new type of speaker, I felt vibrations coming from the device. Thinking of playing video games with my kids, I got the following idea: *Wouldn't it be cool to be able to "feel" the video game?*

• **Research.** To make sure no one had already invented my idea, I went to stores, called speaker companies, searched patent files, and explored the Internet.

• **Prototype and testing.** My manufacturing team built a working model to see if people would enjoy using it. It's important to test every product.

• **Patent.** I applied for a patent so that no one else could use the invention without my permission. This involved describing the invention in words and diagrams with enough detail that someone could build the device. Many books tell how to prepare a patent application. I worked with an attorney to make sure the papers were done properly.

HOW TO Live with Alligators

—by Lynn Kirkland

Alligators and their cousins—crocodiles, caimans, and gharials—have been around for over 200 million years, while the earliest humans appeared only five million years ago! This means that alligators and their kind, known collectively as crocodilians, have lived with people for a relatively short time, geologically speaking. As the dinosaurs disappeared and the Age of Reptiles ended, mammals, including humans, took the advantage and soon *Homo sapiens* dominated the evolutionary scene.

Fast forward a few million years to the present. Crocodilians still play a big role in the natural world. But many species of crocodilians are close to extinction. This time the cause is good old *H. sapiens* (in a word, us).

People who live near crocodilians can learn to coexist with and help these amazing creatures. Even if you live outside "gator country," you can help make sure these reptiles survive. Here's what to do.

DIRECTIONS

1. Help crocodilians:

• *Conserve water.* Crocodilians need water. Water shortages in one place can affect areas far away.

• *Don't buy illegal crocodilian products.* Receive proof that the products were legally obtained.

• *Recycle.* Fewer landfills mean more animal habitats. Compost organic material to reduce waste in landfills.

• *Don't pollute.* Chemicals produced by garbage and other wastes pollute groundwater, wetlands, and oceans.

• *Don't buy crocodilian pets.* Crocodilians generally do not make good pets, and anyone even considering getting one should do some heavy research.

continued ...

2. Live safely with alligators:

• *Don't feed wild alligators.* It's illegal in many places, and it makes gators lose their instinctive fear of humans. They can come to expect food from people after only one feeding. Also, most "people food" is bad for alligators!

• *Keep hands and feet inside when boating.*

• *Don't swim or wade or walk near or along the shore of any unfamiliar body of water.* Assume gators live in any unfamiliar body of water other than a swimming pool. On second thought, check that swimming pool, too!

• *Don't swim or wade in an area where alligators are known to live.* Obey posted warnings!

• *Stay in a group when in or near the water.* Be cautious even in a group, because unwanted alligator encounters can still occur.

• *Don't capture, harass, or tease alligators.* This is illegal. Leave alligator nests, eggs, and babies alone. Young alligators stay with their mothers for up to two years, and female alligators are very protective of their young. A mother alligator guarding her nest and eggs or defending her babies can be dangerous!

• *Walk or run quickly away if you see an alligator on land.* Make sure there's not another alligator in the way! Gators can't move very fast on land—about 11 miles per hour (18 kilometers per hour)—but it's always safer to keep a distance from any wild animal.

• *Keep dogs and other pets from swimming or wading in strange waters.* Watch them while boating.

These tips aren't meant to make alligators seem scary or bad. To live safely with these large predators, we must respect them and give them the space they need. They have their place in nature like every other creature. If you are lucky enough to see a wild alligator, keep your distance, take a photograph, and be glad that you saw it.

Lynn Kirkland grew up in Florida, where she lived among her favorite animals, the reptiles. She's the Reptile Curator at the St. Augustine Alligator Farm and Zoological Park in St. Augustine, Florida.

HOW TO Rescue a Wild 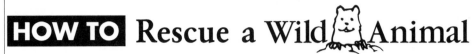 Animal
—by Wildlife Rescue, Inc., Palo Alto, California

Coming across a sick, injured, or orphaned animal is stressful for you and the animal. But there are a few simple actions you can take to minimize the stress you both feel. In the process, you'll increase the animal's chances of survival. The key is to keep the animal warm, dark, and quiet before getting professional help.

DIRECTIONS

1. Find a cardboard box. It should be large enough for the animal to rest comfortably in it, but it should not be so large that the animal can thrash about and hurt itself.

2. Line the bottom of the box with a soft cloth. A piece of flannel or cotton will work fine. Avoid terry cloth because animals can catch their toenails in the looped threads and hurt themselves further.

3. Gently place the animal in the box. Close the top but make sure that air can reach the animal.

4. Put the box on a heating pad set on "low." If you don't have a pad, put a homemade hot water bottle under the box. Wrap the bottle in a small towel first so it doesn't make the box too hot.

5. Place the box in a quiet place. Keep it away from noises emitted by radios, TV, and people.

6. Contact a specialist. Look for a wildlife rehabilitation service or a veterinarian.

7. Do not give the animal anything to eat or drink. An exception would be if you can't get the animal to a specialist for more than 12 hours.

8. Fight the urge to peek at the animal. Doing so will further stress the animal and give it a chance to escape.

RESCUING A BABY BIRD

Many baby birds found on the ground are supposed to be there. "Rescuing" them may reduce their chances of survival. So how do you tell the difference between a bird in danger and one that's OK? It's easy. The starting point is recognizing the three types of baby birds:

• *Hatchlings* are very young birds whose eyes are closed. They may be completely naked or have some sparse down, but no feathers. Hatchlings grow into nestlings.

• *Nestlings* have partially opened eyes (usually in slits), and their bodies are covered with down, prickly looking "quills," or some feathers. Nestlings grow into fledglings.

• *Fledglings* have stumpy tails and are fully feathered, but they cannot yet fly.

What to Do

If you find a hatchling or nestling on the ground, it will need your help. Put the bird in a small box lined with tissue or dead grass. Keep it in a warm, dark, and quiet place. Call a wildlife or animal specialist immediately.

If you find a fledgling on the ground, don't pick it up. When learning to fly, fledglings jump or fall out of the nest and live on the ground for several days, developing their skills. What's more, they aren't alone. Their parents are still around, feeding them, showing them where to look for food, hiding them under bushes, and fiercely protecting them if they're threatened.

Keep dogs and cats away from the area for a few days. If someone picked up the bird, put it back where it was found or under a nearby bush. Don't worry that the mother will reject it because it smells like a human. That's an old wives' tale.

Remember, though: "Over-rescuing" a fledgling turns it into an orphan! But there are exceptions. If it's injured, keep the bird warm, dark, and quiet, and call a wildlife specialist.

HOMEMADE HOT WATER BOTTLE

• Moisten a cloth and place it in a small plastic bag.
• Heat the unsealed bag in a microwave oven for 1 or 2 minutes, or until the bag is warm.
• Seal the bag.

Wildlife Rescue, Inc., Palo Alto, CA is a private organization devoted to helping wild animals in distress and to helping people learn to live with and enjoy wildlife. Working under permits from California Department of Fish and Game and U.S. Fish and Wildlife Service, WRI raises and rehabilitates injured and orphaned wildlife for return to the wild.

HOW TO Ride a Camel

—by Jambaldorj and by Martha Avery

The camel is a peculiar animal, as we're sure you know. From on top, he resembles nothing quite so much as an eccentric armchair. This armchair feels marvelous: it cradles you, front and back, with two great hairy humps, and makes you feel strangely at home. It is a fine place from which to view the Gobi Desert and to think about all the things you have to do that day. We're here to help you do all your camel chores.

DIRECTIONS

1. Milk your camel. People in the Gobi begin each day by milking the female camels. Stand on one leg alongside the camel. Prop the milk bucket on your other leg. While maintaining this slightly awkward posture, put your two arms around one of the hind legs of the camel and get a good firm grip on the camel's teats. Milk by squeezing up and down, up and down. You might want to sing a little bit to keep the camel from getting upset.

Camels give milk all year, which is not usual for animals in Mongolia. It is extremely cold in the Gobi and hard for baby camels to survive, so the mother keeps producing enough food to see her little ones through. A baby camel is nursed for two years, not one, and the great benefit of this is that humans get to drink the milk too.

2. Fetch water. After milking, the next task each day is fetching water. There are wells in the Gobi, but they are often far away, and you generally must ride a camel a distance to reach one. Can you guess the next challenge?

continued ...

3. Saddle your camel. The saddle is made of two layers of rugs. Its stirrups are small, oblong, and light. Mongolian horse saddles, on the other hand, are made mostly of wood; the stirrups are round and very heavy. In Mongolia, people stand up in the stirrups when riding a galloping horse. When a camel gallops, you keep sitting and just rock along.

4. Mount your camel. This is impossible unless you tell the camel to lie down. This is an art that must be learned from an early age in the Gobi, since otherwise you would not survive. Getting a camel to lie down involves chanting to the animal and leading him in circles until he begins grudgingly to buckle his knees and lower himself to the ground.

A camel goes down in the front first, then in the rear. After you've put your leg over him and gently sat astride, he repeats the motion by going up in the rear first, then in the front. This is a rather magical way of being lifted into the air. It feels like the great rocking of a prehistoric animal, lifting you up and back into a time when the world was more stately.

5. Care for your camel. When times are tough, which they often are in the Gobi, a camel can keep itself alive with no water or food for many weeks. It lives off its humps, which are made of water and fat. You can tell a tired and hungry camel by the way its humps sag to one side. The humps of a well-fed, healthy camel are straight and tall. So give your camel time to graze and rest.

6. Shear your camel. Milking, riding, and feeding your camel are daily activities. But there are also seasonal camel chores. Late spring is the time to shear your camel.

The hair that hangs like a beard down the front of male camels is used only for the ropes that hold together a felt *ger*, a round tent also known as a *yurt*. The camel's long neck provides a large area for growing this kind of hair.

On the rest of the camel's body, under a mat of tough hair that protects him in the winter, is the softest, most wonderful cashmere on earth. It's as fine as that of a cashmere goat, but people don't know it because it is mixed with longer hairs. The whole family shears its camels.

We in Mongolia consider the camel a noble but not a sacred animal. If you find a horse skull in the Gobi it is likely to have stones placed inside it as a tribute. Camel skulls never have stones. The camel is not revered, he is simply beloved, perhaps because the animal is a bit like ourselves. He is quirky, easy to trick, but reliable. Most important, like us, the camel knows how to endure.

Jambaldorj is the spokesman for the President of Mongolia. Martha Avery is the founder of Avery Press. She lives in Mongolia and ties her *ger* together with a mixture of camel and yak-hair ropes. Visit the Avery Press Web site: www.halcyon.com/mongolia/AveryHP.html.

HOW TO Survive in the Wilderness
—by Douglas S. Ritter

Looking up, you notice that the light is growing dimmer and realize you better hurry back to camp before anyone starts to worry. You start off.

Suddenly, you realize that you don't recognize where you are. Your heart begins to pound, and sweat beads up on your forehead as you try to remember which way to go. Shadows darken as daylight ebbs away. How could you have gotten lost? What are you going to do?

STOP! Now is not the time for panic. You may not know exactly where you are, but even experienced outdoor enthusiasts become disoriented on occasion. It's nothing to be embarrassed about. Nor will it become a serious problem if you possess knowledge and some basic tools.

The outcome will be determined by how well prepared you are. If you're experienced in the outdoors, before you went off on your hike you took care of a few basics:

• You told someone where you were going and when you'd return.
• You filled your canteen with water.
• You hung a whistle around your neck.
• In your backpack or pockets, you put an empty garbage bag, a pack of matches or other fire starter, water purification tablets, and a folding knife.

Now, some basic survival knowledge can turn the occasion into little more than an impromptu camping trip. In almost any emergency, but especially in a survival situation, it is critical that you follow the four steps contained in the simple acronym S.T.O.P. This acronym gives you a general plan. Specific strategies follow on the next page.

S.T.O.P.

Stop. Take a deep breath, sit if possible, and calm yourself. Whatever happened to get you here is past. It can't be undone. You're now in a survival situation.

Think. Your most important asset is your brain. Use it! Think first so you'll have no regrets later. Take no action, even a footstep, until you have thought it through. In a survival situation, mistakes and injuries occur when we act before we engage our brain.

Observe. Look around. Assess your situation and options. Consider the terrain and weather. Take stock of your supplies, equipment, surroundings, capabilities, and, if there are people with you, their abilities.

Plan. Prioritize your immediate needs and develop a step-by-step plan to deal with the emergency while conserving your energy. Then follow your plan. Adjust it only to deal with changing circumstances.

DIRECTIONS

1. Stay put! If lost, the odds that you will find your way out are slim. If hurt, you'll only make the injury worse by trying to travel. If it's late, you stand a good chance of getting lost in the darkness. When someone notices you are missing, others will start to search for you, such as volunteers and professional search-and-rescue teams.

2. Get shelter and clothing. These items are critical to maintaining normal body temperature. If you're too cold (hypothermia) or too hot (hyperthermia), you can die.

• *Pick a dry location for your shelter.* It should be away from natural hazards. Make do with the best you can find right where you are. Your shelter can be as simple as sitting under a rock outcropping or under overhanging branches of a large tree. However, in a lightning storm, stay away from tall trees.

• *Avoid sitting on the bare ground or snow.* For insulation, sit or lie on gathered small branches or on a downed tree.

• *If you brought a large garbage bag with you, use it to cover yourself and to keep heat in and the weather out.* Cut or tear a head-sized hole in the bottom of the bag, then slip it over your body and stick your head through the hole. Be sure to keep your head out where you can breathe. You can also use the bag as a small shade tarp if the sun is a problem. A cap or hat is always useful to keep your head dry, warm, or shaded, as appropriate.

• *Use a tree, downed tree, or piled-up snow as a wind break.* Curl into a tight ball to conserve heat. If there is more than one person, huddle together for warmth. In hot sunny weather, seek shade. If the ground is soft and you can do so without overexerting yourself, scoop out a hollow. In the shade, it can be 30 degrees F (15 degrees C) cooler 12 inches (30 cm) below the surface.

continued ...

3. Attract attention. The more you can do to attract attention to yourself, the quicker someone will find you.

• *If your shelter is hidden, create a marker pointing to where you are.* Use sticks or some rocks.

• *If there is a clearing, make a big "X" or "SOS."* Form the letters any way you can, by scraping the dirt with a stick, by stomping the snow down with your feet, or by arranging rocks or broken branches and shrubs. Size is vital to effective ground signals. If possible, make the letters 12 feet (4 meters) tall with lines at least two feet (1 meter) wide. Contrast is also important. If the ground is light, make the letters using dark stones or branches. If the ground is dark, look for lighter materials to create the signal.

• *If you hear a helicopter or an airplane, lie down in a clear dry space to make the biggest possible target for those in the air to see.* Always wave wildly with **both** hands in an emergency situation. You don't want to be mistaken for someone giving a friendly wave. If you have something to use as a flag—for example, a shirt—that will be far more effective than your arms and hands alone.

• *Make lots of noise.* Most survivors are found by ground search teams. A whistle is the most effective signaling device. It can be heard for 1/2 to 2 miles (.8 to 3 kilometers) or more in the wilderness, whereas your voice may carry only a few hundred feet (100 meters) at best. The shrill and unmistakable blast of a whistle repeated three times every five minutes is a universal signal for help. It will definitely attract the attention of anyone within earshot. If you hear a whistle, respond immediately with three blasts every time. If you don't have a whistle, you can make a loud signal by banging two rocks together or beating on a dead tree with a stick or rock (but be careful you don't hurt yourself or that the tree or branches don't fall on you if the tree is still standing). *continued ...*

THE TRUTH ABOUT SOS

There are many stories about how SOS came to be the international distress signal, such as the myth that it stands for "Save Our Ship." The truth is that it was selected simply because in Morse code, which was the only means of radio transmission at the time, the symbol for "S" was three short taps and the symbol for "O" was three long taps. Sending this signal was quick and simple. At the receiving end, the message sounded distinctive and was not likely to be missed.

4. Don't fear the night. While the sounds of the wilderness at night may be unfamiliar, there's nothing out there that wants to harm you. If you think you hear an animal nearby, yell, make lots of noise, or blow your whistle. If it's an animal, it will run off. If the noise is searchers, you have been found!

5. Drink plenty of water. In the short term, water is far more important for you than food. It's always a good idea to have at least a quart (liter) of water with you, especially in the desert. The more water you carry, the better. The best place to store water is in your stomach. Don't drink to excess, but if you have water, drink it when you feel the need.

• *If you don't have any water, keep from sweating and breathe through your nose to retain as much water as you can.*

• *Whenever possible, purify water found in the wilderness before drinking.* You can do this using purification tablets or by boiling. However, don't let a lack of purification stop you from drinking from a stream or spring, as long as the water looks reasonably clear. Keeping your fluids at a safe level is more important than the slim chance you might get an illness from drinking the water.

• *Do not eat snow to obtain water.* Snow will make you colder. If possible, start a fire and melt the snow.

The only time the wilderness will bite back is if you panic and forget these basic survival lessons. An unexpected stay in the wilderness is not a big deal if you keep your wits about you. Make yourself as comfortable as possible and wait for someone to find you. No matter how bad your situation, you can be sure others have survived far worse with much less. You must never give up. All you have to do is hold out until help arrives. You can do that. Don't panic. Use your brain. Hang in there. YOU WILL SURVIVE!

DON'T LEAVE HOME WITHOUT THEM

A few inexpensive pieces of equipment are all you need to make survival and rescue more likely, and your unforeseen stay in the wilderness a lot more comfortable.
• A loud whistle (on a lanyard around your neck so it can't be lost).
• 1 or 2 large garbage bags.
• 1 or 2 canteens of water.
• A pocket flashlight (1AA or 2AA size).

Two other items can make a big difference if you know how to use them properly and safely. These tools are considered among the most fundamental survival tools by experienced outdoorspeople.
• A pocket knife: A sturdy, locking folding knife is best and safest. Non-locking pocket knives are accidents waiting to happen.
• Fire starter: Matches, lighter, or flint and steel. These are not toys and can be dangerous and destructive if misused. They should never be carried or employed unless you have received instruction from an adult in their safe use. Once you know how to use these tools safely you should never venture into the wild without them.

IMPROVISATION

Improvisation, the ability to use things for other than what they were originally designed for, is an important survival skill. It's not what things were that's important, it's what they can become, and what they can be used for. Using a garbage bag as a personal emergency shelter is an example of improvisation. Think of your personal belongings and the natural environment as your own private wilderness equipment store. With a little thought and effort, you can improvise everything you need to survive. The five rules of improvisation are:
• Determine what you really need.
• Inventory your available materials, man-made and natural.
• Consider all alternatives before proceeding.
• Select the best strategy that takes the least amount of time, energy, and materials.
• Do it, making sure that the resulting item is safe and durable.

Doug Ritter is an experienced outdoorsman, a pilot, an author, and a survival authority. For more information on wilderness survival equipment and techniques, visit Doug's "Equipped to Survive" Web site: http://www.equipped.com.

HOW TO Walk on the *Moon*

—by Eric M. Jones

It's called "moonwalking," but what you really do is *run*. The Apollo astronauts who landed on the moon (1969 - 1972) found it easy to get their "moonlegs." On Earth, they had practiced for hours walking with complex harnesses to simulate the moon's weak gravity.

But walking on the moon turned out to be harder than expected. Fine, soft dust covers the lunar surface. Walking on it is as tiring as moving across dry beach sand. Also, because the moon lacks air, astronauts had to wear bulky spacesuits that made walking even more difficult.

On the other hand, because the moon is smaller than the Earth, the pull of gravity is six times weaker. When you run, you "float" above the surface six times longer between steps than on Earth and travel six times further. No wonder the astronauts ran from place to place. To share their experience, try the following activity.

DIRECTIONS

1. Put on a spacesuit. Because its gravity field is weak, the moon has no air. You can't survive outside your ship without wearing a pressurized spacesuit. A real spacesuit costs a fortune, but you can simulate one by wrapping sheets of bubble wrap around your legs. Attach the wrap with string. Like a spacesuit, the bubble wrap doesn't bend much and makes running harder. DO NOT COVER YOUR FACE.

2. Find a level place outside. Mark a starting line with a piece of string or chalk.

3. Run forward 12 steps. Have a helper mark the place you reach on that last step. On the moon, you'd cover that distance in two steps!

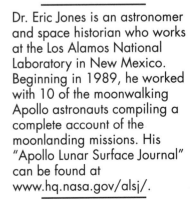

Dr. Eric Jones is an astronomer and space historian who works at the Los Alamos National Laboratory in New Mexico. Beginning in 1989, he worked with 10 of the moonwalking Apollo astronauts compiling a complete account of the moonlanding missions. His "Apollo Lunar Surface Journal" can be found at www.hq.nasa.gov/alsj/.

HOW TO Avoid a Shark Attack

—by George H. Burgess

Sharks are apex predators, the "top dogs" of the marine world. They have a reputation as bloodthirsty killing machines, but this view is distorted. Sharks are not unique in consuming animals. For example, humans are predators, eating cattle, pigs, chickens, fish, and other creatures.

As apex predators, sharks limit the populations of the animals they eat. This maintains the balance of nature. Sharks occasionally do attack humans, but not all attacks are feeding events. Sharks sometimes grab humans by mistake. Other times an attack may protect a shark's space, much as a dog barks at and bites intruders.

The yearly average of unprovoked shark attacks on humans is 75, resulting in about 10 deaths. These worldwide numbers are small given the millions of humans that enter the water. You have a better chance of dying from a bee sting, a dog or snake bite, or lightning than from a shark attack.

DIRECTIONS

To decrease your already small chance of becoming a victim of a shark attack, observe the following rules:

1. Always swim in a group. Sharks most often attack lone individuals.

2. Don't wander too far from shore. Doing so isolates you and places you away from assistance.

3. Avoid the water at night, dawn, or dusk. Many sharks are most active at these times and are better able to find you than you are to see them.

continued ...

THE KIDS' HOW TO DO (ALMOST) EVERYTHING GUIDE

4. Don't enter the water if bleeding. Sharks can smell and taste blood, and trace it back to its source.

5. Don't wear shiny jewelry. The reflected light looks like shining fish scales.

6. Don't go into waters containing sewage. Sewage attracts bait fishes, which in turn attract sharks.

7. Avoid waters being fished and those with lots of bait fishes. Diving seabirds are good indicators of such activities.

8. Don't enter the water if sharks are present. Leave immediately if sharks are seen.

9. Avoid an uneven tan and brightly colored clothing. Sharks see contrast particularly well, so use extra caution when waters are cloudy.

10. Don't splash a lot. Also, keep pets out of the water. Erratic movements can attract sharks.

11. Use care near sandbars or steep drop-offs. These are favorite hangouts for sharks.

12. Don't relax just because porpoises are nearby. Sightings of porpoises do not indicate the absence of sharks. Both often eat the same foods.

13. Don't try to touch a shark if you see one!

14. If attacked by a shark, the general rule is "Do whatever it takes to get away!" Some people have successfully chosen to be aggressive, others passive. Some yelled underwater, others blew bubbles. I personally would go down fighting.

TYPES OF SHARK ATTACK

• **Provoked attacks** are caused by humans touching sharks. Often this involves unhooking sharks or removing them from fishing nets. However, recently there have been a number of incidents involving divers who were attacked after grabbing or feeding a shark while underwater.

• **Unprovoked attacks** happen when sharks make the first contact. This can take three forms.

Hit-and-Run Attacks happen near beaches, where sharks try to make a living capturing fish. In pounding surf, strong currents, and murky water, a shark may mistake the movements of humans, usually at the surface, for those of their normal food, fish. The shark makes one grab, lets go, and immediately leaves the area. Legs or feet are often bitten; injuries usually are minor and deaths rarely occur.

Sneak Attacks take place in deeper waters. The victim doesn't see the shark before the attack. The result can be serious injury or death, especially if the shark continues to attack.

Bump-and-Bite Attacks happen when the shark circles and actually bumps the victim with its head or body before biting. As in the sneak attack, the shark may attack repeatedly and cause serious injury or death.

SHARKS UNDER ATTACK

Although sharks rarely kill humans, humans are killing about 20 to 30 million sharks per year through commercial and sport fishing.

Sharks are blessed with outstanding senses of smell, taste, hearing, and sight; the ability to detect minute changes in water pressure and electromagnetic fields; and other attributes that make them nearly invincible in the sea. Yet they are quite vulnerable to a baited hook and are easily caught. In many areas of the world sharks are becoming seriously overfished and some species are seriously threatened.

More and more people understand that sharks are a valuable part of the ocean environment and must be protected. Fishery management plans have been developed in many areas, but similar action is needed in many other regions. Certain species, such as the white, sand tiger, whale, and basking sharks, have received special governmental protection in some countries.

George H. Burgess is Senior Biologist in Ichthyology (the study of fishes) at the Florida Museum of Natural History, University of Florida. As Director of the International Shark Attack File, he investigates shark attacks. More information on sharks can be found on the museum's Web page at http://www.flmnh.ufl.edu/fish/.

HOW TO Watch a Rocket Blast Off
—by Clarice Lolich

Reading about space travel is fascinating. But for a greater thrill, watch a rocket launch live. It will lift your spirit, and may be one of the most memorable events of your life. Go for it!

DIRECTIONS

1. Pick a launch site. Major rocket bases include: *Tanegashima Space Center* on Tanegashima Island, Japan; *Tyuratam Space Center* in Kazakhstan; *Vandenberg Air Force Base*, Vandenberg, California; and *Kourou Space Center* in French Guiana.

2. Choose a mission. Be aware that launches may be delayed because of weather or technical problems. For schedule information, contact a space organization, or visit the Space Calendar Web site: http://NewProducts.jpl.nasa.gov/calendar/.

3. Study the mission. Important details are: goals of the mission, payload (what's going into space), destination, duration, and the sponsor(s).

4. Bring observation tools. You don't need equipment to enjoy a launch. Rocket engines generate incredibly loud sounds and fiery sights. You can even *feel* the launch as the ground trembles. But if you want to capture the event, bring a still camera, a camcorder, and a tape recorder.

5. Share the excitement. Find a friend who is charged up by space exploration. This will make viewing a launch more rewarding. Ten, nine, eight, seven, six, five, four, three, two, one, BLAST OFF!

SPACE GROUPS
Many of these groups maintain Web sites.
- NASA: National Aeronautics & Space Administration
- ESA: European Space Agency
- CNES: Centre Nationale d'Etudes Spatiales (France)
- CASC: China Aerospace Corp.
- German Space Operations Center
- NSDA: National Space Development Agency (Japan)
- Glavkosmos & Intercosmos (Russia)
- BSC: British Space Centre

Clarice Lolich has worked for many years as an educational consultant for NASA. She has been present at more than a dozen launches, including one mission to the moon.

HOW TO Organize a Bike-A-Thon

—by Christopher Parker

One of my goals is to help people. For example, I take part in a project that sends high school kids on trips to visit colleges so that they will be motivated to continue their education.

To raise money for this kind of project, I organize bike-a-thons: people agree to give money if riders bike a set distance. Sponsors get to root for the riders, and the riders have fun accomplishing a difficult physical task. Organizing this kind of project takes time and effort. But it's worth it.

DIRECTIONS

1. Find a worthy cause. If you care about people, you'll have no trouble finding groups that need help. It's best if you understand the need from a personal point of view. An example is raising money for your school, club, religious organization, or neighborhood. This way, you'll know exactly why the money is needed and how it will be used.

2. Build a team. As you meet people who want to volunteer, keep notes on what they're good at. Valuable fund-raising skills include:
• writing and illustrating letters, flyers, and posters
• using a computer to store information
• getting publicity
• managing security during the event
• preparing and serving refreshments to riders
Hint: Don't ask volunteers to do jobs they don't like or can't handle. If you do, they often will quit.

3. Involve those who will get the money. If you aim to buy equipment for a school playground, ask students to find sponsors and to help during the event. This way they'll feel they earned the money.

continued ...

Mayor, Chris Parker is here to see you...

4. Sign up well-known people to build interest. You don't need movie stars. You'll do fine with the mayor, a business owner, or a star athlete from a local team.

Most celebrities get so many requests, they often don't even answer their mail to say "No." That's why you must meet them in person, for example, at the opening of a park. You can find out when and where by reading newspapers.

Ahead of time, put together an "information handout" that briefly describes your event, why it's important, and the time and date.

When you approach the celebrity, know exactly what you want to say and be brief, for example: "Hello, Mayor ____. My name is Chris Parker. I'm organizing a bike-a-thon to send 100 high school kids to explore college campuses. I'd like your support. Can you ride with us on June 10, or help out in some other way?"

After we talk for a few seconds, I'll say, "Here's an information sheet. Can I call you?" If the person says yes, I'll ask for a phone number.

As you get well-known people to sign up, add their names to the information packet. When one celebrity sees that others have signed up, that may encourage the person to climb onto the bandwagon.

5. Don't handle the money. Too often, money raised for a good cause is mishandled, or even stolen. Many people who would like to contribute need to be convinced that their money will be handled carefully. I find that it's best to get two trustworthy people to manage the money. If possible, they should have accounting experience and they should be well-respected in the community.

6. Have plenty of people on hand during the event. You will need people to guide participants, feed them, make sure the route is clearly marked, answer questions, and so on. If it's a big event, you probably will have to get a permit and work with the police for traffic control. You will also need to have someone in charge of first aid.

7. After the event, share the results with the media. This will help you the next time because people will know that you're serious. Facts to report include:
• how many people took part
• how many total miles were ridden
• how many sponsors gave money
• how much money was raised
Be sure to thank all sponsors. For example, if the mayor took part, go to a council meeting and give your thanks in public.

Chris Parker has organized many charitable events. When not raising money for good causes, he works as a counselor at a juvenile hall.

173

HOW TO Talk to an Extraterrestrial

—by Jonathan Vos Post

If your first meeting with an Extraterrestrial (E.T.) goes well, you will be the greatest hero alive. You could also make a fortune selling your story. But if you mess up, the results could be terrible, perhaps an interstellar war. Feeling a little stressed? Rule Number One: DON'T PANIC! Just follow these simple guidelines, and all will be well. We hope.

If the E.T. was hurt in a UFO crash, or if it's sick, or terrified of you, or intent on injuring you, wait for a team of experts. On the other hand, if you don't have these problems, try making contact by creating and using the planetary coin model described here.

DIRECTIONS

1. Always carry the coins with you. Keep them in an envelope or pocket separate from your usual pocket change.

2. Practice arranging the coins as shown on page 175. Do this outside on a sidewalk or other flat surface. This model features the four inner planets. With a little research, you can create a model of the whole solar system.

3. When you meet an E.T., lay out the coins between the two of you. If possible, photograph and tape all that happens during this "close encounter." At least take quick and carefully written notes.

4. If it's day, point to the coin representing the sun, then point to the real sun and say, "Sun!" If you have your flashlight, focus its beam on the coin so that it is brightly illuminated.

continued ...

MATERIALS
- coins or washers about the sizes shown in the model on the next page
- writing implements
- pocket flashlight
- (optional) a camera, a camcorder, and/or a cassette recorder, film, cassettes, and extra batteries

5. Point to the coin representing Earth, point at the ground around you, and say, "Earth!" Move the Earth coin around the sun coin.

6. If the moon is visible, point to it, point to the coin representing the moon, and say, "Moon!" Move it around the Earth coin.

7. Back away from the coins. If the E.T. knows something about our solar system, perhaps from observation on the way to Earth, it will recognize your model. This will establish that you are an astronomically sophisticated being.

8. Place a handful of coins of various sizes on the ground. Give the E.T. a chance to use them to show what it knows, for example, the positions of the five outer planets (Jupiter, Saturn, Uranus, Neptune, and Pluto). It might place a few pebbles between Mars and Jupiter to show you the asteroid belt. It might even construct a model of its own planetary system. If it moves the coins into a new pattern, record it in written or photographic notes.

Now, if you're lucky enough to encounter an E.T., you're ready to collect information that may be worth billions of times the small change in your pocket.

Jonathan Vos Post is a space scientist and prize-winning sci-fi writer. He is the author of "Me Human, You Alien: How to Talk to an Extraterrestrial," published in *Making Contact: a Serious Handbook for Locating and Communicating with Extraterrestrials*. He is Webmaster of the Magic Dragon Web site, www. magicdragon.com.

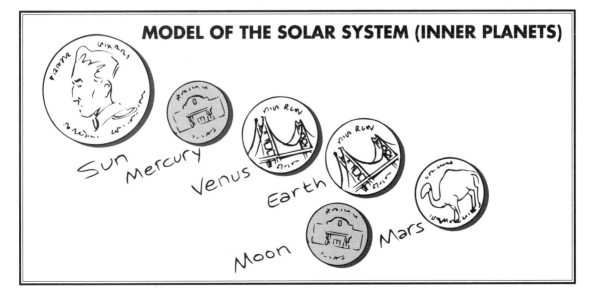

MODEL OF THE SOLAR SYSTEM (INNER PLANETS)

Sun · Mercury · Venus · Earth · Moon · Mars

Index